Spontaneous SUCCESS
is Everywhere

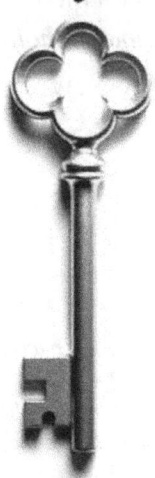

NICHOLAS BOOTHMAN

NICHOLAS BOOTHMAN

Boothman is Dale Carnegie for a rushed era.
The New York Times

Training the New York SuperCops includes daily discussions on the works of Aristotle, H. G. Wells, and Nicholas Boothman
The New Yorker

Copyright © 2024 Nicholas Boothman
The scanning, uploading, and distribution of this book without permission is a theft of the author's intellectual property. If you would like permission to use material from the book (other than for review purposes), please contact info@nicholasboothman.com.
Thank you for your support of the author's rights.

ISBN: 978-0-9958581-3-8
First printing September 2024
9 8 7 6 5 4 3 2

SPONTANEOUS SUCCESS

STOP LOOKING AND START SEEING

When one door closes, another door opens, but often we look so long and so regretfully at the door that closed that we don't see the one that opened.

Alexander Graham Bell
INVENTOR OF THE TELEPHONE

Contents

Chapter 1 A Confirmation	7
Chapter 2 Oh, You Had Plans?	13
Chapter 3 One Door Closes	19
Chapter 4 Another Door Opens	23
Chapter 5 She's Not Angry	29
Chapter 6 Cell Mates	33
Chapter 7 A Flowpath	35
Chapter 8 Benfica	37
Chapter 9 Purpose Over Plans	43
Chapter 10 All The World's a Stage	51
Chapter 11 Shakin' All Over	55
Chapter 12 Desperation is a Mighty Driver	65
Chapter 13 Where Does It All Begin?	77
Chapter 14 Cracking The Code	81
Chapter 15 The Art of Nimbility	95
Chapter 16 She Had Me At Hello	101
Chapter 17 A Carnation Revolution	105
Chapter 18 The Screaming Hill	113
Chapter 19 What Are You Waiting For?	117
Chapter 20 Fate? Or just good luck?	121

Chapter 21 In The Line-up	125
Chapter 22 Who Are You?	129
Chapter 23 How You Do It?	137
Chapter 24 Ben's Story	141
Chapter 25 All It Takes Is A Crazy Idea	145
Chapter 26 Find Your Flowpath	151
Chapter 27 Talk to a Stranger Today	157
Chapter 28 One Thing Leads To Another	163
Chapter 29 Street-Smarts and Common Sense	167
Chapter 30 A Nod From The Universe	171
Chapter 31 A Confession	175
Chapter 32 Diva Ceramica	183
Chapter 33 A Journal	193
Chapter 34 A Holy Man	197
The Spontaneous Success Playbook	209
Acknowledgements	215
About the Author	217

NICHOLAS BOOTHMAN

Chapter 1
A Confirmation

The Bishop's hands, heavy with the weight of tradition and expectation, rested on my head, sending a shiver down my spine as the clock ticked relentlessly towards a quarter to twelve on that cold February day in 1961. My heart hammered a frantic rhythm against my ribs, a stark contrast to the solemn hush of the church, and my voice, caught between boyhood and the precipice of manhood, cracked with the strain of nerves and suppressed emotions. Fourteen and a half, all awkward limbs and gangly height, I knelt there, freshly confirmed into the Church of England, promises echoing in the vaulted ceilings, the offer of a new start hanging in the air like incense. But escape, blessed escape from the suffocating confines of boarding school, was the only thought that truly consumed me.

Boarding school, a stifling world of starched uniforms and meticulously polished shoes, where I spent last night hunched over an ironing board, coaxing creases from rebellious fabric and buffing leather to a mirror shine, all in the desperate hope of eliciting a flicker of pride from the parents I rarely saw. Would they even be here, I wondered, my gaze darting nervously across the rows of unfamiliar faces, searching for a familiar smile, a reassuring presence.

"Today you are confirming the promises your parents made on your behalf at your baptism," the Bishop declared. I sneaked a few peeks behind me. But no mum, no dad, no brother. "In confirmation we are acknowledging we need to turn away from selfishness and accept God's offer of a new start."

What new start?

Half an hour later I was alone on the steps of Saint Michael's Anglican Church wondering why none of my family had come to support me, and more importantly, whisk me away for the day to celebrate the big occasion. Any excuse to escape from boarding school.

Half an hour earlier there had been music and singing and people and glory. Now it was just me feeling stupid, sitting on the steps of the church wondering what to do.

My options weren't great.

And then, the guttural roar of a car engine. A sleek, black beast of a car, its chrome gleaming menacingly in the winter sunshine, screeched to a halt at the bottom of the steps, my Uncle Harry behind the wheel.

"Nicholas." He said, his voice flat, devoid of warmth, "Your dad's dead. Get in."

The world lurched, the ground unsteady beneath my feet. The church, the bishop, the confirmation – all of it dissolved into a meaningless blur, leaving only those three words hanging in the air. Dead. My dad. The news hit me like a physical blow, stealing my breath and leaving me gasping in the sudden vacuum of loss.

He bundled me into the car, the leather seats cold against my skin, the smell of stale cigarettes and aftershave filling my nostrils. Back to school. Back to the prison of routine and rigid expectations. He pressed five shillings into my palm and then he was gone, leaving me standing on the gravel driveway, the weight of the world pressing down on my shoulders.

That evening I bawled my eyes out in the narrow alleyway between the woodwork shop and the gym. I crumpled and hit the walls many times but I held myself up and never fell over. I cried for my dad. I cried for my mum. And I cried for my brother.

I slid to the ground my back against the gym, my feet against the woodwork shop. From high up on the corner of the gym a light cut across my socks and shoes. They were still shiny from the night before. My Dad loved shiny shoes.

"Shoes tell secrets, Nicky," he said, "like a window to the soul." He thought that was funny. "Soul - sole!" I laughed with him.

My shoes. Scuffed, marred by the grit of the alley floor. "I'll fix that before I put them away tonight." And I did.

An hour later I sneaked into the boot-room and polished my shoes. Then, I polished the black school Oxfords of everyone in my dormitory while they were asleep. Then, I mixed them up and put them all back in the wrong pigeon-holes—mine too. Give them something else to talk about in the morning. Give them something to gossip about instead of me.

Even in the face of death, life, it seemed, had a way of finding its own peculiar rhythm. A rhythm that pulsed with a strange, insistent beat, urging me forward, even as grief threatened to pull me under. It was in the silence of that night, in the echoing emptiness of the dormitory, that a question began to take root, a question that would shape the course of my life: what is this rhythm? What is this force that drives us forward, even in the darkest of times? It it some preordained plan, a destiny etched in stone? Or is it something more... spontaneous? Something born of the unexpected, the uncertain, the unknown?

I never got to see my dad again. Never even got invited to the funeral.

Three months later I was gone.

NICHOLAS BOOTHMAN

Chapter 2
Oh, You Had Plans?

I've always been a bit of a rebel, a non-conformist. Never one for the beaten path. Always drawn to the unconventional, the unexpected, the mysteries hidden in the shadows. So when I stumbled upon the concept of spontaneous success, it was like a lightning bolt struck. It all made sense. The ones who truly succeed, the ones who leave their mark on the world, they aren't the ones who play it safe. They're the risk-takers, the gut-followers, the ones who laugh in the face of uncertainty and dance with the unexpected.

Success is often portrayed as a step-by-step climb up a carefully planned ladder. From our parents' dreams for us to society's expectations to work-life balance, we seem increasingly obsessed with planning our lives down to the minute. It's like we're trying to schedule happiness! I'll feel fulfilled from 2 to 3 p.m. I'll feel happy from 3 to 4. But life's not a ladder; it's a weird, wobbly staircase with unexpected landings and surprise detours! Despite our intentions to follow a structured path, unforeseen events, chance encounters, and random collisions frequently alter our course. We can spend hours organizing every detail, mapping out our future step by step, and boom! Life steps in and says, "Oh, you had plans?"

Life doesn't care about your plans. Plans are fragile because life is unpredictable. Life has a way of disrupting even the best-laid plans because, while plans can help organize your efforts, they can't tell you for sure what's going to happen.

Imagine living in a world where everything is predictable; where there is no uncertainty. You wake up, and you don't wonder what the day will bring. You already know. You know exactly what you'll eat, who you'll talk to, what they'll say, and how you'll feel about it. Every single choice you make, you know the outcome before you even make it. No more guessing, no more "what ifs" keeping you up at night.

Making decisions wouldn't be stressful anymore. Instead of weighing pros and cons, you'd just look up the answer. Want to know if that new job is a good idea? Bam, you know the exact result of taking it. Relationships? You'd know exactly how they'll play out, every argument, every laugh, every ending.

But think about it, that spark of excitement when you discover something new? Gone. Scientists wouldn't be exploring the unknown, because there wouldn't be an unknown. And those surprises, good and bad, that make life interesting? Poof. No more.

Maybe you wouldn't feel the need to try so hard, because you'd already know if you'd succeed. Why bother pushing yourself if you know the exact result? And all those big questions about fate and free will? They'd be answered, or maybe they wouldn't matter anymore.

Hope, as we know it, would disappear. You wouldn't need to hope for a good outcome, because you'd already know. And your emotions? Maybe they'd be less intense, less up and down, because there'd be fewer surprises. Time might feel different, too. Would each moment be more precious, or less, if you knew exactly what was coming next? In such a world, where's the room for curiosity, for flexibility, for empathy, or for imagination? And faith? It would become a thing of the past.

Okay, so now forget the world of absolute certainty for a second. Instead, imagine a world where spontaneous success is the norm. Not just a lucky break here and there, but a consistent, almost predictable stream of unexpected wins.

Think about it: you're working on a project, and suddenly, a solution pops into your head, a solution you never even considered, and it works perfectly. Or, you're having a conversation, and you say something completely off-the-cuff, and it resonates with someone in a way you couldn't have planned, leading to an amazing opportunity.

In this world, "planning" takes on a different meaning. It's less about rigid schedules and more about creating the right environment for those sparks of inspiration to ignite. It's about being open to those unexpected moments, trusting that the universe (or whatever you believe in) will provide the right opportunities at the right time.

Careers become less about climbing a ladder and more about riding waves of serendipity. You might stumble upon a hidden talent you never knew you had, or a chance encounter might lead you down a completely different, but incredibly fulfilling, path.

Relationships are built on these moments of unexpected connection. You say the right thing at the right time, not because you planned it, but because you were present and open. You find common ground with people you never expected, and those connections blossom into something beautiful.

The fear of failure diminishes, because you know that even if things don't go according to plan, something even better might be just around the corner. It's a world where "going with the flow" isn't just a cliché, it's a way of life. It's a world where the unexpected is not feared, but embraced, as a source of constant, joyful surprise.

It's important to note that this isn't about recklessly embracing danger or living in a constant state of chaos. It's about finding a healthy balance, accepting that some things are beyond our control, and cultivating a mindset that allows us to adapt and thrive in the face of the unknown. This ability to navigate uncertainty with grace and resilience is a key ingredient to a healthier, happier, and more successful life.

Dreams don't come true in a linear fashion. They flow through your experiences in bits and pieces, with exquisite timing. These moments don't announce themselves with flashing lights, they exist in the margins, in unexpected connections, and in the moments when we choose to see beyond the obvious.

This book's main message is that success often emerges from unexpected places. Rather than relying solely on meticulous planning, it's the ability to pivot and seize spontaneous opportunities that truly unlocks growth. The universe often throws unexpected curveballs, challenging our determination and redirecting us toward unforeseen paths. Yet, it's within these disruptions that spontaneous success is born because we humans are spontaneous beings. What life does care about is the reason you're here, the difference you're meant to make, and the lasting impact you're capable of having.

But what if those curveballs aren't random? What if they're not obstacles to be overcome, but rather, signposts pointing towards a hidden path, a destiny that's been waiting for you all along? What if the universe isn't just testing your resolve, but actively guiding you, shaping you, pushing you towards a future that's more magnificent than you could ever plan or imagine?

And what if that future isn't something you need to find, but rather, something that's already seeking you, reaching back through time to whisper possibilities into your soul?

Are you ready to listen?

Chapter 3
One Door Closes

It was a moment that would change everything.

June 14th, 1967. I was just three months shy of my twenty-first birthday, and I'd just walked away from a lucrative job in advertising. London was behind me, and the open road was calling. I was bound for the Algarve coast of Portugal, where the sun dipped into the Atlantic and the villages were frozen in time.

My mission, shared with three friends, was to open a discotheque in the idyllic fishing village of Praia de Lavanda. But fate had other plans. The local builder, a grizzled man with a face like worn leather and a mouthful of missing teeth, raised his price, and our dream was shattered. My friends chose to return to London, but I stayed, driven by a restless curiosity and the belief that when one door closes, another one opens.

I found a cozy room in a fisherman's cottage overlooking a tiny beach. Every morning, I awoke to the sound of waves lapping and crashing below my window and the chapel bell atop the nearby cliff ringing, signaling that the fishermen had safely returned and it was time to start selling their catch.

The main street, a lazy ribbon of cobblestones, meandered down to the fishermen's beach, where the Hole in the Wall, a ramshackle shop crammed with everything from fresh figs to fishing tackle, doubled as the village post office. Up the road, a sleepy café, its tables shaded by brightly colored umbrellas, offered respite from the sun, while two restaurants, one doubling as a taxi service, promised culinary delights and a ride home. Unassuming doorways concealed hidden tavernas, their enticing aromas of wine, aguardente, and espresso mingled on the cobblestone streets.

Three days into my adventure, I found myself at the Hole in the Wall, a birthday card for my mom tucked into my pocket. The wooden floorboards groaned beneath my weight as I stepped inside, the scent of old paper and olives filling my nostrils. A tall, distinguished man stood at the counter, his pen scratching a signature onto a package. The woman behind the counter, her English halting but her smile warm, beamed at him. "Finally!" she exclaimed. "Today is lucky day, Senhor Tomaz."(In Portuguese, "h" is pronounced like "y").

SPONTANEOUS SUCCESS

"Thank you, Donna Casilda. Your English gets more exquisite by the day."

A short, chunky man in a porkpie hat plonked a case of beer on a shelf and spoke to me. I didn't understand a word.

"I want to send a postcard to England."

The Englishman translated, "Senhor Viera," he said, but Donna Casilda was there in a flash.

"My husband no English," she said, flirting with the Englishman as he left. Then to me as she slipped behind the till, "Postcard to England, eight escudos. Very nice."

As I stepped outside, the man was leaning into the trunk of a gleaming dark blue vintage Oldsmobile, his movements effortless and cool. I approached him, and he looked up, vinyl records scattered around him. With a hint of curiosity, he emerged from the trunk, the records now cradled in his hands.

"Yes?" he asked, his voice low and smooth.

"Hello, I'm Nick," I said, extending my hand.

He took it, his grip firm, and for a moment, our eyes locked. It was a moment that would change everything.

"Thomas," he said, his voice low and smooth.

"I asked him if he lived around here, and he nodded. "Indeed, I do," he replied, "but I have to go." He moved with a fluid motion, closing the trunk, and sliding into the driver's seat. As he started the engine, he turned to me with a warm smile. "Are you perhaps a fan of jazz?" he asked, his voice dripping with theatricality.

"I nodded, and he reached into his jacket pocket, producing a beermat with a flourish. "Ah, Brubeck-type jazz," I said, feeling a spark of excitement.

He grinned, his eyes glinting with amusement. "My new project," he said, as the Oldsmobile roared to life beneath him.

"What project?" I asked, but he was already pulling away.

"Come and see for yourself," he tossed over his shoulder, a challenge in his voice.

I couldn't shake the feeling that I was being drawn into something much bigger than myself.

Chapter 4
Another Door Opens

Back in London, in my advertising days, I'd been a human behavior junkie, trying to decode the secrets of happiness, and selling dreams wrapped in shiny stories. One truth had always stood out: we experience our greatest moments of happiness when we are looking forward to something we want when the outcome is uncertain, that's where the real magic happens.

I was about to experience this phenomenon firsthand. I was happy at the prospect of a night of jazz, and the outcome was certainly uncertain. After a leisurely dinner, I set off to find Thomas' club, Take Five.

The sign was discreet, tucked away in a short, steep cobbled passage between the cafe and the shoemaker's house. A single lantern cast a warm glow around the simple wooden door, beckoning me inside.

As I descended the winding stairs, the sound of jazz drifted up, tantalizing me. But the club was almost deserted, the patrons scattered and sparse.

A couple of locals cuddled up on a sofa in the corner, while a rugged guy with a military haircut fumbled about in a booth. Perched at the bar, a large middle-aged man in a tight suit knocked back Haig whiskey, chatting with Thomas.

I took a seat where I could see the stairs, and a young waiter in a white shirt and black bow tie scooted out to take my order. I asked for red wine, my eyes scanning the room for any sign of what the night might hold.

As I waited, three separate couples arrived, had a drink, and scurried off. A German-speaking family of six groped their way down the stairs, looked around, burst out laughing, and left. The man in the tight suit stumbled off his bar stool and clambered his way up the stairs.

Thomas signaled for me to come and join him at the bar. As I sat down, he smiled, and we found common ground, chatting away like old friends. But I couldn't shake the feeling that there was more to Thomas, and to this club, than met the eye.

When he wasn't changing records, keeping an eye on the waiter, and nodding at the odd new face that poked around the corner, we found common ground and were soon chatting away like friends.

As we spoke, something changed in his voice. It became soft, caring, and kind of mesmerizing. His words felt like a gentle spell, drawing me in with warmth and comfort. He spoke fondly of how a wrong turn had brought him here seven years ago and how he had fallen in love at first sight with a fisherman's daughter called Leonor. And fallen out of love almost as quickly.

"Her family, I'm afraid, are a grasping bunch, with all the finesse of a tornado in a teashop."

Still, even as he recounted the tale of his heartbreak, his voice remained warm and steady.

"We have a daughter, Lara. She doesn't see the world the way I do, but she senses it in ways I can't."

Over the next hour, a dozen or so tourists drifted in, hung around long enough to finish one round, and then left. Thomas looked at me and shrugged it off, but he was clearly disappointed they didn't stay longer.

I had a hunch that the collection of rock, pop, and sweet soul music I'd brought along for the now-not-happening discotheque would be a perfect addition to Thomas's club; it was the swinging sixties, after all. So, I proposed a deal.

"How about you let me DJ here for two weeks, no pay, with a mix of your music and mine, and if the club fills up, you give me a job for the summer?"

"I like things as they are," he replied, his tone firm but weary. He looked around the near-empty room, a hint of doubt flickering in his eyes.

"I love this music too, Thomas," I said. "But it's clear those tourists expect something they can dance and party to. They want excitement. This isn't just about filling the dance floor—it's about energizing the atmosphere."

Suddenly the front door swung open with a clang. All eyes snapped towards the entrance as a tiny, apron-clad figure exploded down the stairs, her rubber boots pounding out an angry rhythm on the wooden steps.

"Tomaz!" she called, her slurring voice slicing through a trumpet solo.

Thomas shook his head, his face a perfect blend of 'oh no, here we go again' and 'I'm so sorry, please forgive my crazy relative.'

"My beloved mother-in-law," he said. "Speak of the devil!"

As the tornado approached, she launched into a rapid-fire torrent of words I didn't understand. Thomas responded in kind, his tone a mix of irritation and embarrassment. Their voices rose and fell, filled with tension and emotion. The few patrons glanced at each other, puzzled and uncomfortable; the trumpet solo now a distant background to the unfolding drama.

The woman's voice trembled with anger as she gestured around the nearly empty club. Then, leaning on the bar top like a crouching tiger, not a foot away from Thomas's face, she spat out in English, "Nobody here! This is dead! Your familia alive!"

With that, she slammed her fist on the bar and clomped back up the steps. Thomas took off after her. Ten minutes later, he returned alone.

He approached me, a forced smile plastered on his face. "Apologies for the interruption," he said, his voice weary. "Family matters. Always... complicated."

But his eyes held a flicker of something more, a hint of fear, a shadow of doubt. What had transpired upstairs? What secrets lurked behind the closed doors of the family quarters?

"Two weeks?" He said.

"Sure," I shrugged, flabbergasted.

"Starting tomorrow?"

"Tomorrow. Sure."

"Deal."

Taking a risk can be a gamble, but this time, it paid off big time. On only the second night, a TV star, entourage in tow, graced the bar with her presence, and suddenly the once-quiet space was transformed into the hottest spot for miles. Word spread like wildfire, and soon a mix of expats and locals, drawn by the promise of glamour and excitement, filled the bar to capacity, making it their new favorite haunt. It was a perfect storm of luck and timing, and before we knew it, Thomas's hidden gem had become a magnet for all sorts of fascinating characters. Tourists, models, missionaries, mercenaries - even monks, their serene presence a stark contrast to the surrounding energy - all converged in this unlikely melting pot. I found myself captivated by the conversations, soaking up stories of faith, wisdom, beauty, and inspiration from spiritual leaders, fashion icons, and creative minds.

And something else. Land was being snapped up by developers and wealthy locals, and lowly government officials somehow managed to trade in their rickety motorcycles for the latest Mercedes-Benz saloons. Foreign tourists by the thousands, looking for all-day happy hours, baking beaches, sizzling sunshine, and all you can eat "spagbol," would soon be galloping over the horizon, waving their flip-flops and phrase books.

The invasion was about to begin.

Chapter 5
She's Not Angry

By the middle of September the visitors had all gone and everything changed. Two years earlier, the first passenger airport at Faro in the Algarve was inaugurated, and what until then was a five-hour winding drive or train ride from Lisbon was now a fifty-five-minute cab ride from the new airport.

Back then, though, sitting in a taverna late one afternoon, just off the main street, I was feeling sorry for myself and trying to figure out where my curiosity would take me next.

I'd polished off a bowl of caldo verde, a traditional thick potato and cabbage soup dished up with slices of chouriço and chunks of freshly baked bread, and was squeezing the last drops of red plonk from a carafe into my wine glass when a rowdy hoard of locals began piling into the main bar to watch Benfica play Juventus of Italy in the semi-finals of the Champions League Cup on the

TV dangling from a chain in the corner. This was a very big deal. The whole country was on edge.

"That will rot your guts." Thomas scooped up my glass and set down a heavy carafe of red in its place. "Try this," he said, as the owner dropped a couple of clean glasses and a plate of potato and codfish fritters between us. He filled the glasses and sat down across from me in front of the open window. It was so bright outside that I couldn't see his face—just a halo around his head from the backlight.

"I can't spend the winter here," I said. "I looked at myself in the mirror this morning and decided I don't want to go back to England just to sell advertising again."

He nodded and looked away.

"Tomorrow morning, I'm getting a lift to Lisbon with Carlos, the Fado guy; he's driving back to finish his military service."

"And who do you know in Lisbon?"

"Actually, no one. Not yet. I'll get a room and see what happens. Like I did here."

"Cheers," Thomas tipped his glass at me.

A commotion broke out across the room. A drunk English woman was yelling at a much younger guy, who was just as intoxicated. She threw some money on the table and shoved him out into the daylight.

"What's wrong with people?" I wondered aloud, baffled by the woman's outburst. "Why does he put up with that behavior?"

"What behavior?" Thomas replied.

"She's angry and being really crude."

"She's not angry, she's afraid."

His words hung in the air. "Fear fuels everything," he explained, his voice taking on a softer tone. "Anger, hate, procrastination, even guilt - they all stem from fear. Perhaps she's afraid of losing him, or maybe she's afraid of being discovered." He paused, letting his words sink in. "You don't know the truth, Nicko. None of us do."

"Instead of judging," he continued, his gaze intense, "try to see the truth. Life's a chain reaction, and every choice we make ignites the next link. Anger or fear? Judgment or truth? The choice is yours."

His words resonated deep within me, but a nagging feeling persisted, a sense that something was amiss, something lurking beneath the surface of this idyllic village.

Chapter 6
Cell Mates

Where do you get this stuff?" I asked.

Thomas's response, when it finally came, was shrouded in mystery. "Five simple words scratched on the wall of a cell." He nodded, his voice soft now, almost reverent, as though what he was about to say was sacred. "Stop looking and start seeing." The words hung in the air like a prayer.

"I shared the cell with a holy man in Hong Kong. His name was," Thomas corrected, "is Raghu. Born in Bombay, to American parents. An astrophysicist, imagine that. But he left it all behind. Went to the Himalayas. Found a link between quantum theory, religion, cosmology... everything. Called it a Flowpath. A way to sense your future..."

"Whoa, whoa, whoa!" I interrupted. "You lost me."

Thomas chuckled. "Yeah, me too, at first. But Raghu, he explained it all. This Flowpath, it's like... a human radar with a mind of its own. It seeks messengers. 'Earth Angels,' he called them. People who can influence your path, even if they're strangers, miles away, or even..." he paused, "...from another time."

Just then, a roar erupted from the bar. Benfica scoring a goal, no doubt. The whole place was on edge, the tension palpable.

"Right," Thomas said, sensing my confusion, "this is neither the time or place." He drained his glass.

I felt like the whole front of my body was a set of double doors, and they were opening up to let fresh air into my soul. I could hardly hear Thomas anymore. I don't know if it was the wine or all the cheering around the TV.

"Up," he said, his voice cutting through the noise.

Up? What did he mean? Where were we going? And who was this Raghu, this holy man who seemed to hold the key to Thomas's cryptic declarations? The questions swirled in my mind, a whirlwind of anticipation and intrigue.

Chapter 7
A Flowpath

There was a big crowd between us and the bar now, and when we got up, the owner just flicked the back of his hand at Thomas from behind the counter. I guess it meant settle-up later.

I followed him down the main street toward the beach. We sat on a bench and stared at the sea. There was no one around; they were all watching the game. The sun was quickly setting, casting glimmering hues across shimmery lights strung between each swaying tree nearby. The square was set up and waiting for the crowd to return and celebrate.

"Seen from way out in space Nicko, this earth of ours looks like a little blue marble rolling around under that sun there," he said. "A tiny, isolated, vulnerable ball of life, hanging in the vast expanse of space, shielded and nourished by a paper-thin atmosphere. In reality, this planet is a single, self-regulating organism where every living thing flows together striving to find an optimum balance for harmony and peace. It sounds crazy, but it's true.

"And us, we are the product of generations before us, a unique blend of genetics and experiences that make each one of us unlike anyone else who has ever existed or ever will. Within you resides the legacy of your ancestors: their achievements and stories. We are the past, carried forward, and we are the future, shaped by that very legacy.

"'Stop looking and start seeing' means shifting your focus from what's missing to what's already present. It's letting go of control and judgment and instead being open to the subtle signs and connections around you. When you do, you'll start to notice coincidences that aren't coincidences, opportunities hidden in plain sight, and beauty in everything."

That was the last thing I remember.

Chapter 8
Benfica

Dark. My head ached. I was alone. Again.

Then, lights. Red and white. I saw them strung along the shore.

People. Music. Loud. Barbecues smoking. Chicken, pork, beef. The smell was thick.

Benfica won?

Donna Casilda. Francesca. Antonio. They waved. "Come here."

Antonio gave me a drink. Aguardente. It burned.

"Ben-fi-ca. Ben-fi-ca." They beat Juventus one-nil. We bounced up and down, cheering. The booze and the conversation flowed. One more aguardente, a plate of chicken Piri-Piri, and fries, and my hangover was gone. Sometime later, I was chatting with an Irish sculptor when a child wearing an oversized Benfica sweater and waving a white envelope tugged at my sleeve. She had the face of an angel.

"Excuse me. This is for you." Her English was impeccable.

"It is?" I got up unsteadily and took it. "Thank you."

She smiled and nodded, her face sweet, innocent, and heartwarming. It was as if she could see right through me.

"Dad wants you to have it."

A fleeting moment of sobriety makes my jaw drop. Could this be Thomas' daughter?

"Are you Lara?" By the time I'd steadied myself and tried to connect the dots, she was gone.

I slumped back down, put the envelope on the table in front of me, and stared at it. Francesca squeezed in next to me. "Mister Nick, I want to thank you for everything you have done for my mother and for me."

After a couple of weeks in the village, I'd made a deal with Donna Casilda. Knowing how much she wanted to speak English, I proposed that I'd teach her English if she taught me Portuguese. So, every day for thirty days, I wrote down ten simple phrases like, 'I can't find my socks,' 'Close the window' and 'Who likes cheese on toast?' Then, after lots of pointing, mumbling, and acting things out, she translated them for me. That way, she learned the phrases in English while I learned them in Portuguese. I made a rule for myself that I had to memorize all ten phrases and throw away the paper they were written on before bed each night. That was three hundred phrases in thirty days. When you can say that much in a foreign language, the rest starts to make sense naturally. Mind you, she drove a hard deal; I had to include Francesca in the lessons.

Suddenly, tears welled up in my eyes and ran down my cheeks. I put my head in my hands and sobbed uncontrollably. I was happier than I could handle. I couldn't remember the last time anyone thanked me for helping them.

Donna Casilda came around to comfort me, but I couldn't stop sobbing. I didn't want to, it felt wonderful. She rubbed my shoulders, and Francesca held my hand. Antonio pushed her away gently and stuck a beer in my hand.

"Ay, Senhor Nick," Donna Casilda said, "What is it the matter with you?"

That's all it took. I got to my feet, hugged them all, still bawling, and shouted out in Portuguese, "It's my birthday, and this is the best party I've ever had. Benfica!"

As dawn broke, we hugged goodbye. The clean-up crew dumped the contents of the tables into garbage cans and carted them off before the wind could have its way with them.

Leaving Lavanda three hours later, I was forever changed. The knowledge and experience I gained during my three-month stay were etched into my soul.

Carlos gunned the souped-up Renault. Blue. Fast. We hit the main road. I looked back. The valley. The village. The chapel on the cliff. When would I be back? If ever.

"Hey. Open that," Carlos said, pointing his racing-gloved hand at the glove box.

I pulled it open.

"That envelope there is yours. Francesca said you dropped it last night."

I reached in and took it out. Sure enough, my name was on it. It seemed vaguely familiar, like a memory on the edge of my mind. I remember a child with a sweet smile, an angel with big, clear eyes wearing a Benfica shirt.'

We stopped to let a group of farmworkers cross the road in front of us. Both men and women were wearing blue overalls, the fabric cut off just below the knees, displaying their purple-stained legs. As they walked, the sound of their flip-flops slapping the pavement made me laugh.

"Grape-stompers," Carlos explained. "They crush the grapes with their feet."

While we waited for them to cross, I opened the envelope. Inside was a single sheet of paper. On it, penned in vibrant turquoise ink, it read:

My dear Nicko, I trust this message brings a smile to your face.

Long ago, in a different chapter of my life, I found comfort within the walls of a Taoist monastery in Macau.

Amidst the serenity, I uncovered remnants of ancient documents left behind by the Portuguese discoverers of the 15th century, who set out on daring voyages to unknown lands like Brazil, India, and parts of Asia. I translated, simplified, and adapted some of the fragments to modern times.

This is my gift to you: The Flowpath, my favorite.

Navigate the currents of life with grace and resilience, embrace the unknown with open arms for there is magic in the unknown.

Find beauty and meaning in the simplest of moments and know that each circumstance that comes your way is part of a perfect plan to transform your purpose into tangible reality.

      Until later,
          Thomas

Chapter 9
Purpose Over Plans

Spontaneous success. Boom. Out of nowhere. Like a lightning strike. One minute, nothing. The next? Everything. But why? Chance? A cosmic dice roll? Or something deeper? Something…programmed?

Is it possible to engineer these moments? To build a success factory? Because if so, I wanted the blueprints. I'd seen too many lives wasted, too many good people grinding their gears, chasing shadows with plans, spreadsheets, rigid structures. Dead ends.

Chasing goals without purpose, blindly following a map drawn by someone else, is like a dog chasing its tail, a frantic, circular pursuit that leads only to exhaustion and disillusionment, leaving a vacuum of emptiness where genuine fulfillment should reside; you might achieve the target, reach the summit, claim the prize, but the reward turns to dust in your hands, a hollow victory that leaves you feeling more lost than ever, because the target itself was flawed, misaligned with your true desires, and your plans, though executed with precision and efficiency, fail to nourish your soul, leaving it starved for meaning, devoid of the values and passions that define you as a human being, making you feel like a well-oiled machine, perhaps, but a machine nonetheless, lacking the spark of genuine life, that nagging feeling, the persistent whisper in the back of your mind, the one that keeps you awake at night, telling you that there's more, that you were meant for something greater, and that whisper, that intuitive nudge, is always right, a constant reminder of the unfulfilled potential that lies dormant within.

Purpose, that elusive force that guides our actions and shapes our destinies, is not a monolithic entity, a singular, universal truth, but rather a multifaceted concept, encompassing two distinct yet interconnected dimensions: life purpose and spiritual purpose; life purpose, the tangible expression of our unique talents and abilities, the specific contribution we are meant to make to the world, is often tied to our natural-born gifts, the things we do effortlessly, the activities that ignite our passion and bring us a sense of deep satisfaction, the very essence of what makes us feel truly alive; find it, embrace it, and you will unlock the key to a life of fulfillment and impact; spiritual purpose, on the other hand, delves into the deeper, more profound questions of existence, the search for meaning and connection, the understanding of our place in the grand tapestry of the universe, the recognition of a force greater than ourselves, the why behind the why, the ultimate reason for our being; these two purposes, though distinct, are inextricably linked, two sides of the same coin, two essential components of a life lived to its fullest potential, and only by aligning with both, by embracing both our earthly talents and our spiritual aspirations, can we truly achieve the kind of success that transcends mere material gain, the kind of success that resonates with the very core of our being, the kind of success that leads to that explosive, transformative, and utterly unforgettable, boom.

Martin Luther King Jr.'s purpose was to achieve racial equality and justice through nonviolent means. To fulfill this purpose, he planned and executed numerous protests, boycotts, and marches.

Serena Williams' purpose is to excel in tennis and empower women athletes. Her plans involve training tirelessly, winning numerous championships, and advocating for women's rights and equality.

John Lennon's purpose was to spread peace and unity through music. His plans involved writing iconic songs like "Imagine" and "Give Peace a Chance."

Albert Einstein's purpose was to unravel the mysteries of the universe. His plans involved years of research and experimentation, culminating in his revolutionary theory of relativity.

These stories are not anomalies. They are proof that when we prioritize purpose, we unlock our full potential.

The Wright brothers' purpose was to achieve powered flight. Their plans involved years of experimentation, testing, and innovation, resulting in the first successful airplane flight.

Malala Yousafzai's purpose is to ensure girls' education around the world. Her plans include advocacy, public speaking, and founding the Malala Fund to support education initiatives.

As a single mother, J.K. Rowling's purpose was to create a better life for her daughter. Her plan involved writing the Harry Potter series, despite poverty and rejection.

Steve Jobs' purpose was to make technology accessible and beautiful. His plans involved creating innovative products like the Macintosh, iPod, iPhone, and iPad.

Their experiences demonstrate how purpose-driven plans can lead to remarkable achievements and lasting impact.

Mark Zuckerberg's initial purpose was to connect college students. His plans evolved into creating a global social network.

Oprah Winfrey's purpose is to inspire and educate through media. Her plans involved creating a successful talk show, founding OWN: Oprah Winfrey Network, and promoting literacy and education.

Page and Brin's purpose was to organize the world's information. Their plans involved developing a search engine that would become the most widely used, Google.

Elon Musk's purpose is to reduce space transportation costs and enable human exploration. His plans involve developing reusable rockets and starships through SpaceX.

By prioritizing purpose over plans, they've unlocked a bounty of unexpected benefits.

Jeff Bezos' purpose is to be Earth's most customer-centric company. His plans involve disrupting retail, cloud computing, and artificial intelligence through Amazon.

The Airbnb founders' purpose was to create a global community of travelers and hosts. Their plans involved developing a platform for unique accommodations.

Beyoncé's purpose is to empower women and marginalized communities through music. Her plans involve creating impactful albums like "Lemonade," advocating for social justice, and inspiring fans to take action.

As they navigated their journeys, they stumbled upon serendipitous encounters that sparked life-changing collaborations. They experienced epiphanies born from unexpected challenges and setbacks.

James Cameron's purpose is to push the boundaries of filmmaking technology. His plans involve directing ground-breaking movies like "Terminator 2," "Aliens," and "Avatar," redefining the sci-fi genre.

In 1938, Nicholas Winton's purpose was to save Jewish children from Nazi-occupied Czechoslovakia. His plans involved organizing Kindertransport, rescuing 669 children and finding them safe homes.

Erin Brockovich's purpose was to protect her community's health. Her plans involved investigating water pollution in Hinkley, California, leading to a landmark lawsuit.

Terry Fox's purpose was to raise cancer awareness and funds. His plan involved running across Canada, completing 3,339 miles despite losing a leg.

Blake Mycoskie's purpose was to provide shoes for needy children. His plan involved founding TOMS, a one-for-one shoe company that donates shoes with each purchase.

Chance meetings opened doors to new opportunities, and synchronistic events aligned their plans with their purpose.

Spontaneity is not just a desirable trait; it's a fundamental aspect of the human experience. In a world where we're constantly striving for control and perfection, it's counterintuitive to suggest that the key to success lies in embracing spontaneity. Yet, the limits of effort and control are clear. When we overemphasize planning and striving, we can miss out on the serendipity and creativity that arises from embracing uncertainty and spontaneity.

When we're spontaneous, we're more open, adaptable, and receptive to new experiences and opportunities. We come alive.

Chapter 10
All The World's a Stage

A sign. A few words. A spark. Suddenly, your spirit ignites. New perspectives. Hidden truths revealed. But are you open? Perceptive enough to grasp the message? Trust those whispers, and the magic unfolds. What was once hidden becomes clear. The unseen, revealed. All the world's a stage, and the answers? Right in front of you. Always have been.

After reading Thomas' letter, a transformation occurred within me. Suddenly, the world seemed to take on a different hue, as if a veil was lifted from my eyes, taking me to another level. It felt as though I'd stepped into the pages of a fairy tale. The street turned into a stage, and the people, with their funny clothes and wine-stained legs, told the story of vineyards, crushing grapes with their feet old-style, crafting the magical drink we joyfully raise a glass to. It felt surreal, as if I was glimpsing into hidden realms where fate and fortune intertwined behind the scenes of life in a next level of vision.

I looked around. It was like the universe itself pulled back a curtain, awakening me to its inner workings. From the subtle interactions between people to the intricate dance of nature's elements, every moment revealed the boundless possibilities that flowed through every facet of existence. I stood at the threshold of infinite potential, where there were no limits to what could be discovered, experienced, and shared.

Moments later, accelerating past the markets, cafes, and the occasional donkey cart, I was overwhelmed with a sense of warmth and security that seemed to envelope everything around me. I was off to start a new adventure, and I would never see the world the same way again.

Carlos and I talked the whole way to Lisbon. I learned that within a month of graduating university, he'd been conscripted into the army. Portugal was at war in Africa.

Winding roads hugged the coastline, revealing stunning views of the Atlantic Ocean. As the landscape shifted from the rocky coastline to the lush forests of central Portugal he treated me to lunch in a roadside chicken shack. I told him how I was in awe of so many of the people I'd met at Take Five. The models, the monks, the missionaries and many of the vacationers; but not the mercenaries. I told him I used to sing in a band.

Five hours later the new Lisbon bridge loomed so brightly that it seemed as if it was alive, pulsing with energy and inviting us to come closer and explore. For me it was a moment of pure excitement. For Carlos, it was back to the barracks.

We crossed the bridge around midnight in silence. When he learned I had nowhere to stay, Carlos sneaked me into his barracks and found me an empty cot. I slept fully dressed, shoes and all. I awoke to a loud horn and guys with shaved heads running past my cot in their underpants. For a moment, I thought I was back in boarding school. Carlos grabbed me, shuffled me past the latrines and pushed me through a small door in the thick fortress walls. "Can you still sing?"

"Sure."

"Then go to the Mexicana and ask for Jose Prazeres. Joe Pleasure. Boa sorte. Good luck." That was it.

The sun was streaming low and golden. I was in love with life, and I was in awe. I was also standing outside a fortress in a strange city, hugging my jacket and knapsack, without a clue where I was. Across the road, a park ran downhill to a monument with a grandiose figure on horseback surrounded by four lions in the middle of a roundabout. A sign on the right side of the park read: "The Ritz Hotel." And beyond it all, in the far distance, the towering statue of Christ the Redeemer welcomed me to the city with open arms.

In my knapsack, a few fresh clothes, an umbrella, a pack of cards, a sewing kit, and my bathroom stuff. In my pockets, a pen, a note pad, a packet of Fisherman's Friends, a Take Five beermat, and one thousand three hundred and sixty-two escudos and forty-two pounds in cash At eighty escudos to the pound, I was worth 8,482 escudos (about 230 dollars back then).

Chapter 11
Shakin' All Over

I made eye contact with the Ritz concierge and said good morning in my poshest English accent. I prayed to find a sign to the men's washroom. I spotted it, right behind the reception. Oh paradise. I needed the washroom in every worst way.

Everything taken care of, including a shave in very hot water and some complimentary cologne, I strolled back into the lobby. It was deserted and the concierge was waiting. I knew he knew I wasn't not a guest so I walked straight up to him and asked how to get to The Mexicana to meet a man called Joe Pleasure. He lolled his head around and gave me the schmuck look. I glanced at my watch, "I realize it's early but..."

"No, no, senhor. It's okay. The Mexicana is a cafe in Praça de Londres? Not very good quality."

He pulled out a blue and white pamphlet and unfolded its thick card cover to show a map. He fondled his pen as if he was about to smoke it and circled my destination. I squeezed a ten escudo note into his hand.

His face lit up and he bowed slightly. "Thank you. Senhor."

"Nick. I'm Nick."

"Mister Nick. Thank-you Mister Nick."

You never know when you need a friend.

Around 8:45 I set off for The Mexicana. Down the street and around the roundabout then up the grand boulevard on the other side. Lisbon's traffic is just a mad race from one set of traffic lights to the next. The Portuguese drive as if they are stock car racers, weaving, yelling, carving up and parking anywhere they feel like. I felt more alive than I had in the last three months in the Algarve. It took me an hour to get there on foot.

All the waiters seemed to know Jose Prazeres. "Mais tarde," they'd say flicking their fingers upwards, "later."

I was on my third coffee and half asleep. When I focused, a young man in a white shirt and rusty brown slacks was sitting in the chair next to me. He looked like a giant chipmunk with a huge mop of black curly hair and thick glasses.

"Mister Nick. I understand you have been looking for me."

"José Prazeres!?"

He pursed his lips and nodded.

"I hear you're looking for a singer."

"That is very possible, but..." He stopped nodding and asked, "Have you ever sung before?"

I wasn't exactly the most attractive kid on the block growing up and I couldn't get a girlfriend, no matter how hard I tried. I was the ultimate loser when it came to dating! But when you really want something, you figure out how to make it happen.

I was walking through school one Friday afternoon, a month after my dad died, minding my own business, when I heard someone talking about this rock band auditioning for a singer, and suddenly it all seemed so obvious.

In a flash, I saw a vision of myself standing on stage, looking out at hundreds of laughing, dancing people, with all my future girlfriends staring up at me lovingly. And I heard this voice in my head: "Hey, Nick, this is it! This is your chance to get a girlfriend." It seemed like a no-brainer, so, in a burst of craziness, I spoke up, "Hey, I want to give it a shot!"

Laughter erupted among the other kids; one of them even had the cheek to say, "Are you serious? Have you ever looked in a mirror?"

It's moments like these that make you question your confidence. I'm six-foot-four with red hair and freckles. Maybe they had a point, but I wasn't going to let a bunch of naysayers get me down.

The lead guitarist's name was Andy. The next morning, the band was in his parent's front room auditioning for a singer. There were six of us trying out; I was the last up.

Andy handed me the microphone and twanged out the opening riff, and right at the spot where I was supposed to come in, I froze. You see, deep down, although I had this brilliant idea for getting a girlfriend, there was just one tiny problem: stage fright. I am terrified. The thought of standing there in front of those people and singing my heart out was paralyzing.

Andy kept the riff going and going, but I couldn't do it even though I'd practiced in the mirror tons of times overnight. It was like there was this plexiglass barrier in front of me. I could feel it. I was right up against it. I could push it, see through it, and bend it, but I couldn't get the first word out. Andy stopped. I was trembling and blushing, but I wasn't ready to disappoint all my future girlfriends.

"Again," Andy ordered. He could look really fierce sometimes, his brows furrowing and eyes narrowing as if he was about to unleash a storm. "Just sing the first line."

I tried again. My hands were clammy and my throat felt tight. I couldn't do it. 'What's stopping me?' I screamed at the top of my inner voice. 'They're laughing at me, and I don't like it. But that's just pride.'

There was a closet next to the fireplace, and I just wanted to crawl inside it and hide. Then I had a brainwave. Why don't I do that and take the microphone in there with me? I figured if I got into the closet where it's dark and no one could see me, I could do it. I ran the microphone wire under the door, squeezed inside, and closed it behind me.

Inside, it was cool and pitch-black, the musty smell of old coats surrounding me. My heartbeat slowed, and I took a deep breath, feeling the microphone solid and reassuring in my hand.

Andy started the riff again, and this time I did it. "When you move in right up close to me," I warbled. "That's when I get the shakes all over me." I sang louder now, getting pumped. "Shivers down the backbone."

Two more lines, and I flew out of the closet like a kangaroo. "Shakin' all over!"

A lot can change in a day, and for me, that day was a turning point. When things seemed bleak, a few simple words sparked a chain reaction of magic moments that transformed my life. I was searching for love, but instead, I stumbled upon a passion for music. I'd auditioned for a band, and before I knew it, I was not only singing but also landed myself a girlfriend - or two!

Music became my refuge, my sanctuary. It helped me navigate the darkest of times, when the world seemed to be crumbling around me. The shock of my dad's passing still lingered, a raw and gaping wound that refused to heal. And the humiliation of being denied the chance to say goodbye, to not being taken to his funeral, it churned me up.

But when I sang, all that pain and anger melted away. The music consumed me, transported me to a place where nothing else mattered. It was my therapy, my escape, my salvation. With every note, I felt my dad's presence around me, his spirit lifting me up, urging me to keep going.

The music helped me find my voice, to express the emotions that threatened to overwhelm me. And with each performance, I felt myself growing stronger, more resilient. The music was my shield, my armor, my protection against the world.

I aced the audition in Lisbon, and soon "A Chave" was born. With Oscar on keyboards, Jose-Luis on guitar, Figueiredo on bass, Cyrilo on drums, Jose Prazeres at the helm as manager, and yours truly, "Nicholas Sharp direct from London," on vocals. We spent the next year and a half living the dream. We traversed the country, playing in clubs, on campuses, recording jingles, and having the time of our lives.

The sun-kissed Algarve coast was our playground for the summers of '68 and '69. José scored three-month gigs at "The Pescador", a swashbuckling nightclub in Albufeira that was the epitome of cool. This two-story nautical wonderland was a treasure trove of fishing nets, lobster pots, and colorful buoys, transporting patrons to a world of maritime magic.

But it was downstairs where the real action happened. Our stage became the pulsing heart of the party, where hundreds of vacationers would let loose and dance the night away. The music was hot, the crowd was electric, and the nights blurred together in a haze of excitement and excess. We were the kings of that summer, and "The Pescador" was our kingdom.

Yet, despite this fantastical existence, a nagging sense of emptiness lingered. Each morning, as I woke up, I couldn't shake the feeling that something was missing. Why wasn't I bursting with joy, eager to start the day? The dream I was living seemed to be lacking a crucial element, leaving me with a hollow feeling that refused to go away.

I wanted to visit Thomas; after all, he was only half an hour's drive from The Pescador, but I knew that would mean I'd learned nothing. I couldn't just seek answers from him; I had to find them inside myself but I barely knew what questions to ask. I needed to read the letter again. For the hundredth time!

I kept the letter inside my lyrics binder. It was backstage at the hotel. I dressed, took the stairs down to the club and found it. The promenade was coming to life. I ordered a milky coffee and hot-buttered toast for breakfast and read it again. The last paragraph said it all.

Find beauty and meaning in the simplest of moments and know that each circumstance that comes your way is part of a perfect plan to transform your purpose into tangible reality.

Beauty, meaning, and circumstances were all around me, everywhere I looked. I could see, hear, feel, smell, and taste them. It started with the toast, then the coffee, then the waves. If I judged nothing, I could hear his voice. Or was it mine?

"I think you know the answer, Nicko." He'd have said. "You're just afraid to face it. But until you find your Flowpath, that emptiness will haunt you, no matter how loud the music plays or how bright the spotlight shines. You're still chasing external highs, aren't you? You think visiting me will bring answers, when the truth lies inside you. So, no, Nicko, don't come visit me until you find your Flowpath."

I knew then that my life was ready to take a drastic turn. The question was, was I ready to face what lay ahead?

Chapter 12
Desperation is a Mighty Driver

The heat is on. Mind explodes. Senses on high alert. Desperation. A mighty driver. Survival instinct kicks in. Suddenly, the world shifts. Insights appear out of thin air. Connections you never saw before. Hidden truths revealed. The impossible becomes possible.

In desperation, there is no comfort zone left to cling to. The familiar boundaries that once defined your sense of security dissolve, and you find yourself standing at the edge of the unknown, vulnerable and exposed. Desperation strips away the your usual safety nets.

I got to know Morgan when she did some work on my farm. As an only child growing up in a dying town, she endured loneliness, and sexual, emotional, and physical abuse.

"I was really unsure of myself and full of shame. What other people said about me used to hurt, especially the really bad stuff."

Morgan allowed me to record her story for this book so that it might serve as an inspiration to anyone else driven by desperation and dignity.

"I used to climb this tree near my house where I could see everything, but no one could see me. One morning, after some really tough stuff happened,—" She trailed off and looked away. "I climbed up to my favorite hiding spot, feeling miserable. I just wanted to keep climbing and escape everything. But then this voice in my head—I don't know if it was my own or what—told me that if I stayed there, I'd never make it out alive. So, while they were out, I grabbed a bus to a women's shelter I'd read about 15 miles away."

"A few days after I arrived at the shelter, Melissa, the woman in charge, handed me a magazine. She pointed out an article and said I should read it. It was about a guy from England who climbed trees for a living and spent most of his childhood doing it. I got choked up because it felt like the universe was sending me a message. I mean, here I was, reading about trees in a magazine made from paper that comes from trees. It sounds crazy, but I was in a tough spot and I grabbed onto this wild idea. If this guy could turn his passion into a career, why couldn't I?"

"I landed a job at a cafe near the shelter and worked hard to be the best waitress I could be. Melissa had told me that no matter what you're doing, always give it your all because people are watching. So, I made sure to be super efficient, friendly, and always looked put-together. I saved every single cent and tip I got, and I didn't spend a dime. I got my meals at the cafe and got essentials like soap from the shelter. Finally, I had enough to rent my own room. With a real address, I signed up for a forestry class at night school and started reading this book called 'Introduction to Forestry and Natural Resources'. I was in control of my life and it felt amazing!"

"You must be so proud of yourself." I said. " I can see the determination in your eyes."

"About a month into my forestry course, something really strange happened. One of my regular customers at the cafe asked me if being a waitress was my dream job. I thought he was joking, but then he handed me his business card. Across the middle, it read Wyatt's Tree Service—Removal, Pruning, and Planting. But it was the tagline that touched me: I Nurture Nature's Beauty.

He told me he'd noticed me studying my forestry textbook during slow periods at work. I was surprised he'd even noticed!

I told him my plan.

"He told me that the book was a decent starting point, but I'd need tons of hands-on experience to really learn the trade. It felt like a kick in the stomach. I got that same old feeling of being completely helpless, like I was going to be sick. But then he said he could use someone to help run his office and that he'd teach me the ropes."

Today, Morgan and Wyatt have a four-year-old daughter and a busy year-round business nurturing nature's beauty. Morgan recently spearheaded a service to provide farms and tree nurseries with their leftover wood chips to improve the soil quality around the roots of new trees and help them retain moisture.

Morgan is a testament to the importance of consequential strangers and of listening to your inner voice. If you're desperate and in need of help, it's natural to seek assistance from others. However, it's important to exercise caution and ensure that the people offering help are genuine and trustworthy. Here are a few ways to navigate this situation:
- Evaluate their credibility. Look for indications that

they have the knowledge, expertise, or experience relevant to your situation.
- Trust your gut. Watch out for warning signs like conflicting details, unreasonable requests, or a lack of openness.
- Start with small steps. This lets you assess their ability to follow through before relying on them too much.
- Get a second opinion. Make sure they have your best interests in mind: not just theirs.

Tough times can surprisingly bring some good stuff your way. When you're going through a rough patch and drop all your usual guards and judgments, you can end up reaching out for support and advice from books, coaches, friends, and sometimes the heavens. And sometimes, out of nowhere, serendipity drops by.

In late 1969, I married a young South African woman I'd met in the Algarve. At the beginning of October, our daughter was born, and in the middle of November, with the promise of a job from a family friend of my new wife, we flew to South Africa—on one-way tickets. But the reality was far from glamorous. It turned out what the friend meant by "a fashion marketing executive" was actually me driving around the African countryside, flogging ladies underwear and leather gloves from the trunk of a car! No way. Our room was paid up until the end of the month but with only two hundred pounds and no tickets back home, we were stuck.

I felt like I'd hit rock bottom. But as I sat on a bench outside our rooming house the next morning, something shifted. To my left was a hardware store, its window display a jumble of tools and hardware. To my right was a newsagent, its shelves stacked with newspapers and magazines. But it was the banner in the corner of the hardware store window that caught my eye: "Blossoms Bring a Sparkle to the Summertime Air."

And in that moment, something clicked. I had an epiphany, a spark of inspiration that would change everything. It was as if the universe had sent me a message, a reminder that even in the darkest of times, there's always hope. And with that hope, a new journey began.

Just before leaving Portugal, I was fascinated by some huge paper flowers I saw in a furniture store window. My curiosity got the better of me, and I went in to check out how they were made.

When the newsagent opened at six, I bought sixty sheets of brightly colored tissue paper in an assortment of shades. When the hardware store opened at seven, I bought twelve thin green garden canes, a roll of green gardening tape, three yards of stiff gardening wire, and a pair of strong scissors. I took a ten-inch and a twelve-inch vinyl record from a lopsided stack of cardboard boxes in the hallway next to my front door (records to the rescue once again!). Using them as templates, I made twelve sample flowers.

That morning, I hitchhiked into Cape Town.

I stuck out my thumb, and fate intervened. A sleek sedan pulled over, and I slid into the passenger seat. The driver, a well-dressed man with a kind face, introduced himself as a former city councilor. We chatted as he navigated the roads into Cape Town.

As I shared my predicament, he nodded thoughtfully. "You're looking to sell those paper flowers, eh? Well, I've got some advice for you. There are only two places to sell them at this time of year: Garlicks and Stuttafords."

He glanced at me, his eyes sparkling with insight. "Those are the only two department stores that might be interested. And even then, no guarantees."

Now, I had a mission. I would track down Garlicks and Stuttafords, and I wouldn't leave until I'd sold those paper flowers. The question was, would I succeed?

I wangled my way to the homeware buyers at both places. Garlicks ordered twelve dozen. Stuttafords, twenty-four dozen. At five rand (the South African currency) apiece, I stand to make more than two thousand rand. Back then, the average apartment rent was around a hundred and eighty rand a month. Now all I had to do was make them.

On December 2nd, I cadged a lift from a friend of my wife, and delivered the flowers in person. By January 15th, we had our own apartment, our first and last month's rent paid, and enough furniture to eat and sleep in peace in a trendy neighborhood.

Beautiful 'synchrodipity,' but I never want to go through that again.

In February, I cut my hair, bought a suit, and talked my way into a job selling advertising space with the Cape Times, the city's morning newspaper. On the first day, the boss called me into his office, took a feature section out of his filing cabinet, opened it on his desk, and spun it around so I could take it in.

"Twice a year, we bring out this fashion supplement, but the advertisers don't like it." he said. "You're young, so I want you to go out there and find out why."

Without thinking, I piped up. "I can tell you why right now. The pictures are dreadful; I can take better pictures than that."

"You think so." He looked me right in the eye.

SPONTANEOUS SUCCESS

Back in my advertising days in London, I was indoctrinated into the mantra "Ready, Fire, Aim!" - act now, figure it out later. And bang! It just went off in my head.

"Yes."

"For sure?"

"Yes."

He made a quick phone call, then said. "OK. You're on." Just like that! What had I gotten myself into? I didn't know the first thing about photography.

With the help of the newspaper's fashion editor, I found the best models in town, the best hairstylist, the best make-up artist, the best stylist, and a seasoned wedding photographer with his own studio. I confided my innocence to the stylist and she discreetly told me every good move she'd ever seen a photographer make.

When the 16-page supplement was published the following Saturday, it included a small text box in the center of the opening spread that said, "Photos by Nick Boothman."

On Monday evening, my phone rang.

"Hello Nick. This is Sydney Baker. I'm the fashion editor at Fair Lady Magazine. I saw your pictures in the Cape Times, and I'd like you to shoot a spread for us."

Fair Lady was the most popular women's magazine in all of South Africa at the time.

Busted!?

"Oh, that's great, thanks," I said, desperate to get out of this because I didn't actually take the pictures, I just told the models what to do and the photographer took the shots, "but I'm really busy."

"Well, dear, we shoot three months ahead, so I'm sure we can make it work."

Jeepers. Now what? "And I'm very expensive." I said turning up the heat.

"Listen, love," Sydney came back, "we're not the best payers in the world, but we want you to shoot eight pages, and we pay three hundred Rand a page."

A huge flash went off in my head. At the time, I am earning sixty-five Rand a week. I think he just offered me about six months wages for a day's work.

Ready, Fire, Aim!

"Ok. That's great." I said still in shock.

"I'll be in touch." He said and hung up.

Now what?

We were living in a suburb of Cape Town called Wynberg. I walked past the Wynberg Pharmacy every day on my way to the train station and I remembered seeing used cameras for sale in one of their windows.

That afternoon I got off early and headed for the pharmacy.

I told the guy at the counter I was doing a photo spread for Fair Lady magazine and I needed a camera. I guess he thought I was a nut-case but in the end he sold me a used twin-lens Rolleiflex and told me to read the manual and the instructions inside the film box. That was the end of the paper flower money.

The shoot was a big success thanks to the heaven-sent stylist from the Cape Times shoot, and because the model we chose was a gem. Upbeat, beautiful, and humble, nothing was too much trouble. "Want to try it again?" she'd say. "Let's try it this way."

The following week, I quit my job at The Cape Times and rented a studio two blocks away from Fair Lady's offices. It was the start of a 25-year career as a fashion photographer with studios on three continents

Desperation is a double edged sword. It can creep up like a thief, stealing your sense of security and replacing it with gnawing anxiety. It can be a raging fire that consumes you, or a spark that ignites transformation.

In that moment, I discovered the secret to Spontaneous Success. It's not about waiting for the perfect opportunity or until the stars aligned. It's about embracing the desperation that drove me, and using it to fuel my journey.

Chapter 13
Where Does It All Begin?

A few years ago, I was sitting in my car in a Home Depot parking lot near my farm in Canada with a young friend. We're listening to a discussion on the radio about caffeine. A so-called expert said, "It's virtually impossible to give up caffeine cold turkey."[1]

The kid looks at me, a flicker of something in his eyes, almost relief and says, "See. That's why I can't quit."

A statement, not a question. A declaration.

I say, "Why?"

I wanted to see where he'd go with it.

He says, "Even the experts say it's impossible."

Ah. The experts. The convenient excuse.

I say, "What nonsense."

Not loud. Not angry. Just a quiet dismissal.

There's a concept in psychology called Locus of Control, which is essentially how much control you feel you have over your life. If you have an 'internal locus of control', you tend to believe that you can control your outcomes and destiny. If you have an 'external locus of control', you tend to believe that pressures outside of you control your life and destiny.

He was leaning heavily on that external locus. It's a common thing. Easier to blame the outside world than to take responsibility.

It wasn't about the caffeine, not really. It was about the mindset. About the way he saw himself.

People like to give away their power. They find comfort in believing they're at the mercy of forces beyond their control. But that's a dangerous path.

Because even in the smallest things, there's a choice. A decision. And those choices, those decisions, they add up. They define you.

The kid in the truck? He had a choice. He just didn't see it. Or maybe he was afraid to. And that, in a way, is a kind of tragedy."

As we grow older, it becomes clear that we always have a choice in life. It's like this big neon sign flashing in front of us saying, "Hey, you're in charge!" When you start dodging those choices, you're actually relinquishing responsibility and choosing to let other people or circumstances call the shots on your destiny.

Here's the thing about responsibility: It's all about being able to respond and take control. The moment you start pointing fingers, blaming others, or making excuses for what's going on in your life, you've just handed over the reins. You've given up your ability to respond. When you start playing the blame game, that's it. You're stuck. You might not realize it right then and there, but you're stuck like a fly on flypaper.

"Sorry I'm late for work. It was the traffic, the weather, or my alarm!"

No it wasn't. You didn't plan properly. If you blame the traffic, the weather, or your ex, what's going to happen next time?

At times, when we're stuck in a mindset where we believe things won't improve for us, we tend to blame ourselves and adopt a victim mentality. This traps us in feelings of unworthiness and perpetuates the victim mindset, making it impossible to find a way forward on a Flowpath.

NICHOLAS BOOTHMAN

Chapter 14
Cracking The Code

My time at Take Five was brief, but it was long enough to leave a lasting impression. As I observed the people around me, listening to their stories and struggles, I started to pick up on something fascinating. There were patterns of behavior, subtle habits and mindsets, that seemed to make all the difference in their journeys.

These individuals, who'd opened their Flowpaths, shared certain characteristics. They had a way of moving through life that was smoother, more effortless. It was as if they had cracked the code, unlocking the secrets to a more harmonious, more fulfilling existence.

I became obsessed with understanding these patterns, with teasing out the underlying principles that made them work. And as I delved deeper, I began to see that these behaviors weren't just random traits - they were essential components of a larger system, a system that could help anyone find their way onto their Flowpath.

Here are 10 examples you can try to help you crack the code and find your own Flowpath

1. Speak Up

It can be scary to insert yourself and express your opinion, but when you speak up, others notice you, what you stand for, and what you have to say. When you don't speak up, you remain invisible.

Professor Thomas Harrell at the Stanford Business School spent twenty years looking for "success factors." His research revealed the number one identifiable predictor of future success across all areas to be something he called "social extroversion": the ability to speak up. This is an ability we were all born with! It's just that some people don't do it because they're afraid to. Perhaps they've had "the rules" drummed into them growing up. "Don't talk to strangers," "Only speak when you are spoken to," or "Stop asking so many questions!"

Hesitation and the inability to speak up are luxuries you cannot afford when you're making new connections.

So how can we overcome these barriers and learn to speak up or take action without hesitating?

With the three-second rule.

2. Use The Three-Second Rule

The three-second rule is the ultimate spontaneous success tool. It works for anything that tempts or scares you, like when you're considering talking to that stranger sitting next to you on a flight, when you're thinking about speaking up at work, or even when you're psyching yourself up to ask someone out on a date.

Here's how it goes: You spot someone you want to chat with, and instead of overthinking it and getting all tangled up in your thoughts, you count in your head, "One, two, three." Boom! And just like that, you make your move. No thinking, no hesitating. You stride right on over there and introduce yourself, say something interesting, or maybe throw a question their way. It's all about taking action right away.

The crucial part is the timing. You've got to do it within three seconds. This rule helps overcome the brain's natural resistance to change by building momentum and confidence, and overcoming fear and self-doubt.

That's the magic window. Don't let your brain start going, "Hey, wait a minute, what if they don't want to talk to me? What if I embarrass myself?" No, shut that voice down. The three-second rule is all about bypassing that noise and going for it. Trust your gut and embrace the moment.

Practice in the Playbook

3. Stop Trying, Start Doing

The next time you catch yourself saying, "Oh, I'll try to do that," stop right there. Take a step back and reassess. Are you really going to try, or are you going to do it?

"Try" is a tricky little word. It's like a get-out-of-jail-free card for not really committing to anything. It's a safety net—a built-in excuse for not giving it your all.

If you want to motivate yourself or others, you've got to ditch the "try" mentality. It's all about action, about going all in with no hesitations. Don't just try; do it. Give it your best shot and don't let that little word "try" hold you back.

I know this seems like a picky distinction, but as you read on, you'll realize the importance of self-talk, not just to your conscious mind but to your unconscious mind. J. K. Rowling didn't say, "I'm going to try to be a great writer." She grabbed her pen, her paper, her baby, and her ideas and roamed from café to café around the streets of Edinburgh and got on with it. Mother Teresa, Martin Luther King, Oprah Winfrey, Ray Charles, Barbara

Walters, Tiger Woods, Margaret Thatcher, Richard Branson, and Lady Gaga didn't say, "I'll try." They grabbed their ideas and ran with them. Not one of them will tell you it didn't come without hard work. Not one of them will tell you they didn't ache, agonize, practice, and polish their talents, knacks, and attributes every moment of every day.

The same advice applies to words like must, should, ought to, etc.

4. Turn Off The Blame Game

The blame game is a linguistic villain lurking in the shadows, ready to sabotage our lives. In a study called Blame Contagion, researchers Will M. Hart, John F. Dovidio and Samuel L. Gaertner determined that people who love pointing fingers and blaming others end up losing status, earning less and performing worse. It's like a self-destruct button they've unknowingly pressed. What's more, blame doesn't just mess with your success; it also snatches away your chances for positive change.

Blaming others is no big surprise. Listen to your friends, neighbors, and the media. We are surrounded by helpless language. "The politicians are to blame." "Blame it on the unions." "The doctor says it's impossible." "Life's too short." "It's Monday!" "Obesity is a disease." "He's shy." "It is what it is." "It's Friday—what do you expect?" "My ex is a complete jerk!"

I overheard this conversation recently. "My boyfriend's angry with me. He blamed me for getting a speeding ticket, but it wasn't my fault; it was my boss's fault for making me work late. And the cashier at the supermarket, too. If she'd been organized, I'd have been out of there in good time. And the cop. Couldn't he see my stupid car could never go as fast as he said?"

Is this someone ready to open a Flowpath? There's no mystery about how to get out of the blame game. Listen out for negative, helpless, and blaming language. Let it trigger an awareness in yourself to monitor your own thoughts and words until you can remove blame and excuses from your thinking.

5. Cultivate Confidence

Cultivating confidence empowers you to explore new ideas, challenge your existing beliefs, and take risks.

If you look closely at confident people, you will find they are not afraid of failure. They know there's no such thing as failure: there's only feedback. One of the most important lessons in life is to learn from your failures. It's okay to mess up and to fall, but what's not okay is to stay down. When you fail, process feedback, get back up, and change what you do until you get what you want. And again. And again. And each time, you will learn something new that will bring you one step closer to success.

Keep telling yourself, 'There's no such thing as failure, only feedback,' until it becomes a part of your truth.

Confident people are not afraid of rejection, either. They know there's no such thing as rejection; there's only selection. One of the main reasons people are uncomfortable reaching out socially is the fear of rejection, but it's a mistake to look at it this way. Rejection isn't personal; it's part of the natural selection process. You wouldn't walk into a car showroom and buy the first car you saw. Instead, you'd start your new car "project" with a general idea of what you want, then try out a few models until you found one that felt right. Most of the ones you'd reject would be perfectly fine automobiles for someone else—just not you. You go through the same process of selection when buying a new outfit, a home, or just about anything else of importance to your life.

Keep telling yourself this too, 'There's no such thing as rejection, only selection,' until it becomes a part of your truth as well.

6. Find A Sunny Disposition

A "sunny disposition" refers to a cheerful, positive, and optimistic attitude. People with a sunny disposition are often resilient in the face of challenges and have a contagious ability to uplift those around them with their positive energy.

Optimism plays a crucial role because it creates a fertile mental environment that is open to new possibilities and insights.

Dr. Martin Seligman describes a condition in his classic work, Learned Optimism, where some humans have learned to behave helplessly despite having numerous opportunities to help themselves.

Consider this. A pessimist walks down an alley, and an apple drops on his head.

"See! Bad things happen to me all the time, wherever I am," the pessimist says to himself. "I'm unlucky."

An optimist walks down the same alley, and an apple drops on her head.

"Some idiot dropped an apple on my head," she mutters to herself, and that's the end of it.

What's happening here?

The clue is in time, place, and taking it personally. The pessimist is saying to himself, "Bad things happen to me all the time, wherever I am. I'm unlucky." There's no wiggle room there. The optimist's self-talk is quite the opposite. Not all the time, no particular place, not my fault.

7. Become A Temporary Optimist

When you approach life with optimism, you are more likely to notice patterns, make connections, and experience those magic moments, but hey, if you can't do that you can become a temporary optimist instead.

Here are some stats published by Time Magazine in late 2021.

- Optimists are 40% more likely than pessimists to get a job promotion in the next year.
- Pessimists report feeling stressed about money 145 days more than optimists in any given year.
- People with a positive style are 13% less likely to have a heart attack than those with a negative style.
- 80% of the human population is inherently optimistic.
- Optimistic men and women are more than 50% more likely to reach age 85 than their negative counterparts.
- Pessimists are five times more likely to get burned out than optimists.
- Optimists are six times more likely to be highly engaged at work than pessimists.

So, whistle and sing happy tunes to yourself for a few minutes every day and watch your life transform for the better.

8. Take Smart Risks

Dealing with risks is crucial for anyone who wants to be confident, happy, and engaged with life. "To grow, we need to experience challenges, whether we're 4, 14, or 40," says Dr. Michael Ungar, a professor at the School of Social Work at Dalhousie University in Halifax, Nova Scotia. In his book Too Safe for Their Own Good, he warns that today's society has become risk-averse. "By bubble-wrapping our lives," says Dr. Ungar, "we are taking away opportunities to experience the building blocks of growth—which may be the biggest risk of all."

There are a lot of things that can hold us back: fear, self-doubt, or just not knowing where to start. It's easy to get bogged down in those feelings and let them keep us from trying new things.

In 2020, I spoke to a room packed full of engineers at The Venetian, the biggest hotel in Las Vegas. The topic was Risk and Rapport by Design, a speech about rallying and inspiring customers and employees.

Marcus, a man in his mid-forties, is sitting in the second row. I ask him if he believes he can go out into the Piazza San Marco and introduce himself to three strangers in five minutes.

"Not a chance," he laughs. "Never."

"What if I offer you a hundred bucks?"

"Not a chance. Not for five hundred."

"Do you have a partner?" I ask.

"Yes."

"Heaven forbid," I say, "but if someone kidnaps your partner and will only release them if you introduce yourself to fifty new people in ten minutes, could you do it now?"

"Of course," Marcus says. "That's completely different."

Risk is relative. Your imagination can conjure up images of things that scare you, or it can be used to inspire you to act with great courage. The choice is yours.

Trust Yourself: Remind yourself that you have the ability to make good decisions. Practice non-judgment and see for yourself.

Practice in the Playbook

9. Practice Non-Judgment

Judging events and circumstances on a Flowpath is like applying the emergency brake while you're hurtling down a freeway. By learning non-judgment, we free ourselves up to pursue magic moments without restriction. My response to new people, events, and circumstances has always been "I wonder what this is all about?" or "Good luck, bad luck? Who knows?"

That said, while non-judgment promotes flow, avoiding judgment completely can cause problems. If we don't use some judgment, it's hard to figure out if something is harmful, or see when we need to judge a situation for practical, ethical, or safety reasons. Finding a balance is key. It means we can enjoy the good parts of being non-judgmental while still handling important situations wisely.

10. Release The Past

Before embarking on the next chapter, consider the power of forgiveness. Forgiveness liberates you from emotional burdens and enables you to see situations from different angles. Holding on to grudges and resentments only serves to slow flow.

Releasing the past does not mean erasing its existence or pretending it never happened. It's about relinquishing the grip of anger and resentment that have dragged you down for far too long and instead choosing to set foot on the path of progress.

Forgiveness, often seen as a sign of weakness, may, in fact, be one of the most formidable acts we can undertake. Consider this: what if forgiving someone is the key that unlocks our own liberation? What if, by pardoning the wrongdoings of others, we grant ourselves the freedom to forge ahead, unchained from the ghosts of the past?

Yet, let us acknowledge that there are certain wounds too deep to mend, certain transgressions that inflict irrevocable harm. In such instances, forgiveness may seem unattainable or require a significant passage of time. Additionally, some may struggle to forgive, unable to release the grip of anger and pain, or due to a perception that the wrongdoer fails to comprehend or accept the weight of their actions.

We all stumble at times, and we bear the weight of remorse for actions that haunt our conscience. Yet just as crucial is the act of forgiving ourselves. In granting forgiveness, we grant ourselves the liberty to do our own thing and embrace the untrodden path of our lives. For if we hold on to grudges and refuse to forgive, we shall forever remain prisoners of those who have wronged us.

Chapter 15
The Art of Nimbility

Nimble. Pivot on a dime. Adapt. Cat-like. Curveball. No problem. Shift. Adjust. Improvise. Obstacles and opportunities. Dead ends and detours. The unexpected? A chance to shine. Winners and wannabes. What's the difference?

My career as a fashion photographer was a wild ride, filled with crazy shoots, impossible deadlines, and more twists and turns than a bestselling thriller. But looking back, I realize that those chaotic experiences were secretly sharpening my skills in the art of Nimbility.

I learned to expect the unexpected on set. A sudden rainstorm would soak the models, a tardy model would throw off the entire schedule, or a wardrobe mishap would leave us scrambling. But that's where my Nimbility kicked in, allowing me to think on my feet and conjure up creative solutions faster than you can say "flashbulb."

When my Flowpath demands quick decisions, I rely on my trusty Nimbility to guide me. It's like having a built-in Ready, Fire, Aim! response, where I take action first and then adjust my aim based on the outcome. This mantra is etched in my brain: prioritize swift action over perfect planning.

In a world where the only constant is change, Nimbility is the ultimate superpower. It's the ability to stay one step ahead of the curve, to pivot when necessary, and to always land on your feet. And trust me, it's a skill that will serve you well on your own Flowpath.

Sara, a 27-year-old fax machine sales manager, is the queen of the Ready, Fire, Aim! approach.

Faced a pantyhose predicament under the Florida sun. She didn't like the panty lines or the seam that showed through her open-toed shoes, but she did appreciate the control top's benefits. Then she had a brainwave.

Using scissors, she cut the feet out of a pair of control-top hose and wore them under her pants. "That's when it hit me," she says, recalling the magic moment. "That's how Spanx came to be."

Sara quit her job and spent the next two years and $5,000 of her savings visiting clothing manufacturing plants up and down North Carolina for research.

Modeling her creations herself, she persuaded Neiman Marcus to carry Spanx. Bloomingdale's, Saks, and Bergdorf Goodman followed.

Forbes Magazine named Sara Blakely the youngest self-made female billionaire in the world and one of Time Magazine's 100 Most Influential People in March 2012.

"Every person in their life has had a million-dollar idea," Sara says. "The biggest difference between a successful idea and a failure is whether or not you get out and take action."

Facing a massive order from Neiman Marcus without ready inventory or production, she boldly said, "YES!" and then figured out how to make it happen.

When Oprah included Spanx in her "favorite things" of 2000 and wanted to film Sara's office, Sara had no office to showcase. Unfazed, she again said, "YES!" and promptly established an office, staffing it with a team.

Since its inception in 2006, the Sara Blakely Foundation has donated millions to charities around the world, focusing on those that empower underserved women and girls.

Sara's magic moment mantra: "Say YES! and then make things happen."

Arthur Ashe, the legendary American tennis player, had his own version of Ready, Fire, Aim! His magic moment mantra was "start where you are, use what you have, and do what you can."

Arthur began his tennis career in an era where racial barriers were prevalent. He didn't have access to the same resources or opportunities as many other players due to racial segregation. So, he started where he was—despite these challenges—and made the most of what he had. Additionally, he did what he could within the circumstances. He focused on his game, constantly improving, and advocating for equality in tennis. His dedication, perseverance, and commitment to social change went beyond the tennis court.

Start Where You Are: Instead of waiting for the "perfect" moment or circumstances, you can start taking steps toward your goal immediately, using the resources and skills you currently have.

Use What You Have: You might not have access to all the resources or knowledge you think you need. Nevertheless, by focusing on making the most of what you do have and tapping into your imagination, you can leverage your resources effectively.

Do What You Can: Instead of getting overwhelmed by the magnitude of your goal, break it down into manageable tasks. Take action on the things that are within your control.

With this philosophy, Arthur Ashe won three Grand Slam titles in singles and two in doubles. He was the first African American player selected to the United States Davis Cup team, and the only one ever to win the singles titles at Wimbledon, the US Open, and the Australian Open.

Serendipity, that magical dance of chance and fate, often unveils its most enchanting moments in the realm of "love at first sight."

Love at first sight embodies the principles of spontaneous success, involving an instant connection, unpredictability, effortlessness, passion, purpose, a project, and a Flowpath.

Dr. Earl Naumann, author of Love at First Sight, interviewed and surveyed 1,500 individuals of all, races, religions, and backgrounds across America, and concluded that love at first sight is not a rare experience. What's more, Dr. Naumann theorizes that if you believe in love at first sight, there's a roughly 60 percent chance it will happen to you out of the blue. Here's what led him to that conclusion:

Nearly two thirds of the population believe in love at first sight.

Of the believers, more than half have experienced it.

Fifty-five percent of those who experienced it married the object of their affection.

Three quarters of these married couples stayed married.

Sometimes though, things don't work out as you hoped. One minute we're cruising along, thinking we've got it all figured out, and the next, everything changes. For me, that change came a year later. In February 1972, my marriage ended, and I left Cape Town and moved back to Lisbon. In the midst of upheaval, I discovered a new opportunity. I opened a fashion photo studio on the top floor of a stunning building in the heart of the city I knew so well, and a new chapter of my life began to unfold. I moved between my studio in Lisbon and soon another in Madrid, and with my ability to speak Portuguese, business flourished quickly, and my entrepreneurial spirit skyrocketed.

Then came the biggest surprise of my life.

Chapter 16
She Had Me At Hello

When I opened my fashion photo studio in Lisbon one name kept popping up while I was doing the rounds with my portfolio: Wendy. She had modeled for Yves Saint Laurent in Paris, danced with the Royal Ballet in London, owned her own plane, owned the model agency in Lisbon, and everyone seemed to know her. All that and she was only 25 years old. I was getting fed up of hearing about Wonder Woman Wendy everywhere I went, and before long, "Miss Perfect" was at the top of my list of people I didn't want to meet. Nevertheless, when I needed three kittens playing with a basket of wool for a magazine cover shot, my inner rascal couldn't resist contacting her classy agency. The receptionist asked me to hold, and a few moments later a voice came on the other end: "Hello, this is Wendy."

"Hi. My name's Nick Boothman, and I'm a photographer."

"Yes, I know," she replied softly.

"Whoa!"

It turns out that she wanted to meet in person this crazy English photographer she'd been hearing about who had shown up out of the blue in Lisbon.

That unexpected encounter was the start of a spontaneous success story that changed my life forever.

The moment I met her, I found myself drawn to her in ways I couldn't explain. When our hands touched inadvertently while leaning over to arrange a prop for the kitten shoot, I felt a rush of energy come up through the ground, and I heard myself say, "This is the most ridiculous thing I've ever said in my life, but I love you."

An orchestra inside my head had been going like crazy since the moment she walked into the studio and introduced herself, but it suddenly stopped. Wendy was looking straight at me. "Oh my God," she said eventually. "What are we going to do now?" I knew she felt the same way.

We've been together ever since, raising five children and still deeply in love. It was as if the universe brought us together in that instant—and we knew it.

Every moment, every choice we make, sets off a chain reaction of consequences. From the moment we wake up in the morning to the time we lay our heads down at night, we are in a constant flow of causes and effects.

Acknowledging that life is a chain reaction reminds us that our actions, no matter how small they may seem, have the potential to set off a series of events that can shape not only our own lives but also the lives of those around us.

Day-to-day hangouts for spontaneous stimulation are everyday spots where you can meet new people and spark fresh ideas. Think coffee shops for casual chats, parks for a change of scenery and creativity, and community centers or libraries for events and workshops. Fitness classes and gyms not only boost your mood but also help you network, while bookstores can ignite new interests. Local markets and street fairs are full of vibrant energy and new connections, and even online communities can lead to spontaneous collaborations. These places make it easy to stumble upon unexpected opportunities and inspiration in your daily life.

The trouble is that today, technology is isolating us from these vital sparks. There's something about the experience of walking through a shopping center, playing games with real people, flipping through a print publication, or listening to the radio that you can't easily duplicate online. When you walk around a department store or mall in person, even if you only came in for one thing, you can end up stumbling on all sorts of cool stuff and collecting random experiences you won't find online. Play games outdoors instead of online and you find a whole world of adventure waiting for you that takes your breath away. Pick up a newspaper or a real magazine, and you'll discover loads of interesting stories and fun facts from all over the place. Listening to the radio is full of surprises; you get your favorite songs mixed with new ones you've never heard before.

Nowadays, we rely so much on technology to find exactly what we're looking for that it snuffs out our natural curiosity, empathy, imagination, and sense of exploration—things we're naturally wired for.

Chapter 17
A Carnation Revolution

On April 25th, 1974, in what became known as the Carnation Revolution, military officers who opposed the authoritarian regime that had run Portugal for forty-eight years carried out a military coup. Overnight, Portugal swung from one political extreme to the other, and work for this English fashion photographer, who had moved to this little corner of paradise seven years earlier, dried up. Amidst the uncertainty and upheaval, I found myself at a crossroads, but a chance encounter set off a chain reaction that changed everything.

There I was chatting with a stranger at the local English ex-pat pub near my apartment when he turned out to be the recently arrived head of immigration at the Canadian Embassy in Lisbon. Initially, when he suggested to a group of us ex-pat Brits that he could get us out to Canada, we laughed. Brazil? Same language and exotic, yes. Spain? Right next door and exciting, yes. Canada! You must be joking. But he was right.

A week later, on a whirlwind trip to London to break the news to my mother about my move to Canada, fate took a mischievous turn. Stepping off the sidewalk, I collided with a man on a folding bike, clad in a sharp three-piece suit topped with a classic bowler hat.

"Good grief! Nick Boothman. What the hell are you doing in London? I thought you'd disappeared with the drunken hoards in Portugal." Ross always spoke as if he was addressing a thousand people. He'd been my boss in the advertising department at Woman Magazine seven years earlier.

"Actually, I spent two years in Portugal singing in a band, then two years in Cape Town, plus another three years back in Portugal as a fashion photographer," I told him. "But Portugal's gone through a revolution, so I'm moving to Canada to make a fresh start." I squashed the last seven years into a few minutes.

"Well," he said, still straddling his fold-up bicycle, "you must come and meet Cousin Bernard. He's over from Canada, and he's coming to dinner tonight. Mad character, but lots of fun." He reached into his vest pocket and handed me his card. "Office at home these days."

And so, that evening, I found myself in the company of Cousin Bernard, who turns out to be the senior menswear buyer for Eaton's, a century-old Canadian department chain with more than 200 stores across the country.

Back in Portugal, it took a while to complete all the medical exams and paperwork, but, at 1:30 pm on Friday, August 15th, 1975, I boarded Canadian Pacific Flight 223 from Lisbon to Toronto with one thousand and sixty US dollars, the maximum allowed by the currency restrictions imposed by the new government, and one third of a ton of excess baggage. I was twenty-nine.

In Portugal, I'd made a handsome income as a fashion and advertising photographer. That morning, though, I bid farewell to my four-bedroom apartment by the ocean. Twelve hours later, I was washing my socks in the sink of a one-room unit in a Toronto rooming house.

I made a list of my resources. Hasselblad cameras, flash meters, a portfolio, a healthy body, a goal, a payphone in the corridor—first and last month paid up, six hundred dollars left—and one hot contact. Cousin Bernard.

At 9:30 am on a bright Toronto morning, I went to the payphone and called Cousin Bernard.

"Hi. Remember me? Nick Boothman. We had dinner in London."

"Yes. I think so." He sounded frosty. "This is not a good time. Call me back in a couple of weeks. Goodbye."

Ouch. When I met Cousin Bernard in London, he offered to introduce me to Eaton's whole advertising department. He boasted that they turn out more than forty pages of newspaper and magazine advertising every day—all photos. I was counting on Cousin Bernard.

Two days later, while exploring downtown and making cold calls to advertising agencies, something didn't feel right. The weight of uncertainty settled in the pit of my stomach, and a voice in my head said, "Call him again." So, from a payphone outside Toronto City Hall, I called Cousin Bernard again.

"Hells bells and hallelujah!!! Where are you? I thought you were some idiot pant rep I met in London. Where are you? Right now?"

"I'm near City Hall in front of the Sheraton."

"Don't move. Stay right where you are. Not an inch!"

Five minutes later, Cousin Bernard came sprinting down Queen Street and wrapped his arms around me. "The second I put the phone down I realized what I'd done." He said. "Holy Mackerel. We tried everything to find you."

"Come," he said.

It's only 11:15, but Cousin Bernard whisked me off to the bar on the top floor of the Sheraton for a very long, boozy lunch. For starters, Cousin Bernard, a very passionate Canadian, had me down a "Red Beer," beer with tomato juice, and a "Bull Shot," vodka with beef stock and Tabasco. We ate, drank red wine, and planned until five, when he staggered off to catch the commuter train home.

The next day was dedicated to parading me and my portfolio around Eaton's art department. Cousin Bernard must have had some sway there because I got my first full-day shoot the following Tuesday. We shot cruise wear. Two full pages in black and white for the back pages of all the national newspapers.

My pictures cause a small scandal.

Around Europe, I'd been shooting extreme high-fashion with a twist of shock value; why not? It worked. But very conservative Canada wasn't quite ready for my style. My very first full-page newspaper ad caused a scandal. By 10 a.m., Eaton's closed its PR department due to the volume of complaints. The feminists and social activists from the Royal Commission on the Status of Women publicly chastised the Premier of Ontario.

And I learned a new word: sexist.

On the other side of the coin, Eaton's sold out, and everyone wanted to know who shot the ad. My new career was made overnight.

So, let's tally this Flowpath of magic moment messages:

Busy fashion photographer in Portugal: revolution; work dries up; bump into an immigration officer at my local pub; decide to go to Canada; bump into a man on a bicycle in London; meet Cousin Bernard; arrive in Canada; two weeks later, busy fashion photographer again.

Spontaneity at work?

Some of you might be nodding, thinking, "Yep, that was synchronicity right there!"

Others might be raising an eyebrow, whispering, "No, no, that's definitely serendipity."

And then there's another group scratching their heads, going, "Nah, it's all just a bunch of coincidences, right? No big deal." And perhaps there's truth to that.

I also like what Agatha Christie, the world's greatest mystery writer, says about this.

"I've often noticed that when coincidences start happening," she said, "they go on happening in the most extraordinary way. I dare say it's some natural law that we haven't found out."

NICHOLAS BOOTHMAN

Chapter 18
The Screaming Hill

In March 1979, Wendy and I purchased and moved into a big house in Toronto with our three children. We were living the dream, or so it seemed. But as the years went by, the pressures of success, the stress of providing for a growing family, and the emptiness of material pursuits started to take their toll. Despite the outward trappings of success, I couldn't shake the feeling that something was missing. Even as I achieved more and more, the sense of fulfillment and purpose seemed to elude me.

It was only when we took the bold leap, seven years later, to leave behind the comforts of our city life and embrace the simplicity of a farmhouse on 130 acres that I began to grasp what had been eluding me. We exchanged a grand house in the heart of Toronto for a more rustic existence, trading material possessions for the promise of a more authentic life. "Wendy had found a safe place for us and our children. It was friendly, quiet and calm, surrounded by nature. We hiked, swam, hung out, camped on the grounds. And we rode our horses. But the move came with a steep price: my photographic career and our dwindling savings, which vanished quickly with three children in university and two in nearby schools. But this time, I'd learned a lot about starting over.

In 1998, I became seriously ill. The whole family was frightened. Surgery followed, as did many treatments. The children told Wendy, "Mummy, we'll be okay. You focus on getting Daddy better."

Wendy established a rule: "there will be no weeping and no sadness around Nick." At 5 p.m. every day, we held 'happy hour' and opened a bottle of red wine. She told visitors that only positive talk was allowed. But one day, she needed to explode. She drove up the hill to a spot with a 360-degree view, where the whole family often went for picnics, got out of the car, banged on the ground with her fists, and screamed.

On her way back, a huge stag stood on the hill, staring at her. It didn't flinch as she passed. Wendy felt the stag was saying, "It's all going to be okay."

From that day on, whenever anyone needed to scream about anything, they'd go up to that spot. Even friends would call to ask if they could go up there and scream. That's how the spot got its name: The Screaming Hill.

And life, as I've learned, has a peculiar way of testing our resilience. Just four months later, I accepted an invitation to speak about my work as a photographer at the North York Camera Club in Toronto.

Little did I know that this seemingly ordinary event would be the catalyst for a series of extraordinary events that would challenge my newfound philosophy and push me to the very limits of my understanding.

But was I ready to unlock the door?

NICHOLAS BOOTHMAN

Chapter 19
What Are You Waiting For?

"How can I make this event interesting?" I wondered. "I know, I'll talk for five minutes about photography and fifty-five minutes about connecting with people." When I finished, three people came up to me: a doctor, a teacher, and someone who teaches people-skills to airline personnel. "Can you come and give this talk to my staff/students/teams?" they each asked. "Not the photography bit, the rest. The connecting with people part."

That night, I told Wendy, "I'm going to be a speaker." When I woke up the next morning, she asked me, "Do you still want to be a speaker?"

"Passionately."

"What makes you think you've got what it takes?"

"Well... I guess I have a way with words."

"You can be very persuasive." She said. "What else?"

"I'm pretty fast on my feet."

"So you're persuasive and flexible. What else?"

"I think I've found a fresh way to approach a popular topic."

"So, if you were hired to do a photo shoot of a speaker with an audience, what would you do?" She asked.

"Simple, I'd book space at a local hotel, hire an actor, and invite a bunch of people to come and listen."

"So, what are you waiting for?"

By noon, I'd rented half of the ballroom at our local Holiday Inn and invited a bunch of friends, clients, models, and advertising agency friends to come and hear me talk about Rapport by Design, a souped-up version of the talk I gave to the photographers.

"Twenty-nine bucks a head," I told them, "and bring your friends." Over eighty people showed up. I was buzzed. Now I was a professional speaker—but it was going nowhere, and because I'd pushed my photography aside, my income had taken a nosedive.

What was missing? I researched what makes other speakers successful, and it hit me like a champagne cork. A book! And preferably a best-seller with a killer title. I'd never written anything coherent in my life, but that wasn't going to stop me. I burned a bridge, so I couldn't go back. I traded in my cameras for a laptop and started to write—but I didn't have a clue where to start, and with three kids at university and two at high school, things soon got desperate.

Six weeks later, all the optimism in the world couldn't disguise the fact that we were running out of money. What have I done? What have I put my family through? What was I thinking? Our little corner of paradise was turning into hell.

One misty morning, I stood on the Screaming Hill, enveloped in silence. And then, as if carried by the gentle breeze, I heard Thomas whisper in my ear—clear, distinct, and unforgettable. The stillness seemed to amplify his message, making it resonate deep within me: "What's missing, Nicko, is a purpose. You're living the dream, but is it truly yours? Or is it just a distraction from the void inside you? You're chasing dreams and love, but have you considered what truly fulfills you? What sets your soul on fire?"

In that moment, gazing out at the rolling hills and fields, I knew I stood at the threshold of discovering something far more profound than the success I had left behind. The real magic lay not in external achievements but in uncovering my true purpose and passion.

The words hung in the air, a gentle prompt to awaken to the truth I had been seeking.

Later that night, I made a deal with myself. I had to write 1500 words a day before I could get dressed. For the next five weeks, I wrote with a vengeance and completed the first draft of How to Make People Like You in 90 Seconds or Less, a book with a purpose. To make complicated concepts sound simple and interesting.

Chapter 20
Fate? Or just good luck?

On the inside, the big old 1870's wooden peg-barn on the farm where I live, looks like a bootlegged medieval cathedral. It's over sixty feet from stable to gable and it has appeared in movie and fashion shoots, country music specials and music videos.

On the third Saturday in October of 1998, ten days after I finished the first draft, our grand old barn hosted an exhibition of historic quilts. This has been planned almost a year earlier. The highlight of the event is a collection made from the clothing of one of the greatest storytellers in recent history--Lucy Maud Montgomery, the author of the international classic Anne of Green Gables.

Over three hundred people showed up. By seven-fifteen, the last visitors are gone, and we are shutting down and locking up. A car carrying four passengers crunches up the gravel driveway and stops in the courtyard. Inside are two middle-aged couples who have driven out from Toronto and got lost—this is before GPS. We turn the lights back on and give them a quick tour.

As the evening wound down, we invited them to join us for a glass of wine. To our surprise, one of the group turns out to be the president of a famous Canadian publishing house. The woman, her eyes sharp, her voice carrying the weight of authority. The president of a publishing house. Fate? Or just damn good luck?

Before saying goodbye, this gracious lady extends an invitation for me to visit her office the following week. There, she offers invaluable advice, urging me to seek representation from a reputable agent in New York. With her guidance and a stroke of luck, I embark on a journey that leads me to a six-figure advance from a major publishing house a mere three weeks later.

At first, these surprise twists and turns are mind-blowing. It's like fireworks going off, painting your life in all sorts of colors that make you stop and think, "Wow, anything can happen." Every chance connection and fortunate coincidence feels like fate giving you a nudge, showing you how much potential there is in your life. But as time goes on, you start getting used to this unpredictable dance. What was once mind-blowing now becomes a regular part of your day. The amazing things start feeling ordinary, and the everyday stuff takes on a new kind of importance. You learn to go with the flow of life, understanding that each random meeting or unexpected event adds another layer to your story.

After getting used to it, you realize the magic isn't just in the big, mind-blowing moments. It's in the everyday stuff too. Those routine moments that you might have overlooked before now carry the potential to change everything. The small, subtle things keep shaping your path, and even though the surprises become more familiar, they still have the power to steer your life in a whole new direction. It's not about the shock and awe anymore; it's about recognizing the silent, ongoing influence of these moments in crafting the story of your life.

And as I stood on the precipice of my new understanding, a single question echoed in my mind: What surprise was waiting just around the corner?

NICHOLAS BOOTHMAN

Chapter 21
In The Line-up

In March 2001, a Canadian organization named WRED, Women and Rural Economic Development, contacted Wendy and me to develop a program that would uncover women's hidden strengths. We'd spent three years developing a project designed to cast off constraining beliefs and reveal liberating natural-born strengths in men and women. We called the project Purpose Quest.

But were we ready? Were we ready to step into the spotlight, to become the guides, the mentors, the champions of change? The weight of responsibility settled on my shoulders, a mixture of excitement and trepidation. This was more than just a project. This was a calling.

The quest revolves around the Parable of Purpose. It goes like this:

Imagine, in your mind's eye, that a few moments before you are born, you find yourself in a line-up with a slip of paper in your hand. On that paper, you have to write, in one short phrase, the reason you deserve to be born. The only condition is that it has to be something of benefit to humanity, because we know humanity evolves over time. Let's call this your Purpose Statement.

This scenario obviously isn't real. It's a parable, a made-up tale told to teach a lesson or share a moral message, so it's easy to remember and relate to.

When you get to the front of the line, the powers-that-be look at your slip of paper and either say, "Not good enough; go back and try again," or else they say, "Great, very good; you can get born."

Armed with your Purpose Statement they send you over to the "To-Be-Born Supply Department" to be fitted out with all the attributes and talents you'll need to accomplish your purpose.

Depending on what you've written, they might grant you patience, caring, courage, humor, organizational skills, eloquence, a flair for languages, drawing or music, etc.—whatever you'll need.

Once you are filled to the brim with your attributes and talents, you are ready to be born. But here's the catch: just before you leave, the powers-that-be tear up your slip of paper and wipe your conscious memory.

And so you enter the world with an unshakeable sense that you were meant for more. You may find yourself drawn to certain professions, or certain causes, without quite knowing why. You may have a talent or a skill that seems to come naturally, without any formal training. All the while, that sense of purpose burns within you, driving you ever forward, even as you struggle to understand what it all means.

So, here you are, knowing deep down that you are uniquely equipped for something, but you haven't a clue what it is. Not consciously, at least.

By the time you reach the end of this book, you'll uncover the unique message inscribed on your metaphorical slip of paper: your Purpose Statement. With this newfound clarity, a path will begin to emerge, and you'll become increasingly aware that life is no longer something that happens TO you; it's something that happens FOR you.

This parable is not some airy-fairy, magical-thinking, idealistic notion cooked up to make you feel warm and fuzzy inside. No, your Purpose Statement is the cold, hard truth of your natural-born potential in your everyday existence. It's a message that's unique to you and intended solely for your own use. It serves to keep you focused, stimulated, and on track, as you'll soon see. That said, while it feels good to know your unique purpose, it's just words until you start doing something with it.

Revealing raw talents and attributes is tricky because it involves people being able to describe themselves accurately. Knowing we'd found them? Easy. A fountain of joy springs forth. They straighten up, their eyes sparkle, their skin tingles, and their faces fill with excitement as tears of joy and relief stream down their cheeks. They undergo an undeniable and profound epiphany.

Chapter 22
Who Are You?

If someone asked you to describe yourself, what would you say? Most people find it tough to give an accurate answer. And can you blame them? Other people have been labeling us since the day we were born. "You're so smart." "You're shy." "Why are you always so clumsy? Depending on other people's ideas about who you are is a recipe for failure.

Ask someone to give you seven words to describe themselves, and you'll soon figure out that they can't quite do it, at least not accurately. For instance, they might say they're "caring," "creative," and "organized," but if you delve deeper, you might find that when they say "caring," they actually mean "vigilant." When they mention "creative," what they're truly talking about is being "resourceful." And when they use "organized," they might actually mean "methodical."

This may seem like splitting hairs, but a caring, creative, and organized person is not the same person as a vigilant, resourceful, and methodical person. This becomes more obvious when you look at the negative words people use to describe themselves. Words like "I'm shy," "I'm 'negative', and "I am 'antisocial." You weren't born that way. If someone believes these descriptions of themselves, just imagine the catastrophic consequences of decisions made based on these false beliefs. How can anyone take the fast track to spontaneous success if they're not sure who they are to begin with?

A young firefighter named Jackson once told me he was shy. His mother called him shy when he was growing up. "Oh yes, Jackson's such a shy boy." "Oh, Jackson. Stop being so shy!" Well, jeepers. Hearing this over and over, the seeds are sown. When Jackson takes the Purpose Quest and discovers there's no such thing as shyness—that it's not a natural-born attribute—and that he's actually "cautious and reserved," which are good things, his negative self-esteem stops holding him back, and he's able to move along a different, stronger path.

"People say I'm negative," Mehdi, a sound engineer, explained. "I'll be in a meeting and someone comes up with a great idea, and I get mad that I didn't come up with one myself."

I pointed out that he was probably defining "competitive" and not "negative." He was relieved to get closer to his true self.

The truth is, there's no such thing as a negative attribute; only positive ones turned upside down by time and circumstance.

After a speech I gave in St. Louis, Emilie came up to me and said, "When you mentioned that bit about living in a world where millions of introverts are forced to masquerade as extraverts just to make a living and it doesn't come easy, you were so right. I planned this event tonight, and I'm an introvert—I'm totally anti-social."

I told her I didn't believe there is such a thing as anti-social. "I'm guessing," I told her, "that you were probably born super-sociable. And when you were young, someone hurt you so badly in your 'super-socialness' that you turned that attribute upside down and said no one is ever going to hurt me like that again. On the bottom of the attribute was written 'anti-social' but deep down, you are still super-sociable."

"You are right." She hugged me with happy tears.

A troubled woman in her late thirties, Susan, attended one of our Purpose Quest workshops. She lived on her husband's family farm, thirty miles north of Toronto. It was her duty to cook, clean, shop, and wait on her in-laws—mother, father, brother, and uncle—as well as help them out around the farm when things got hectic.

Susan was at her wits' end: insecure, depressed, and anxious. We began by telling her it was okay to not feel okay. It really helps to allow yourself to feel whatever emotions are coming up.

"Everywhere I turn, I'm marooned," she said. "I don't know whether to go forward or backward, left or right. I don't know which way to turn."

When asked to come up with seven words to describe herself, she snapped, "I'm an aggressive, angry bitch for starters. Or so I'm told." She eventually added: methodical, loyal, challenging, and impatient.

An hour later, we had accurately reframed the words she gave us to describe herself. When we dug deep down, aggressive became stimulating, angry became quick-witted, bitch turned into having high standards, and impatient changed to ambitious. The rest stayed the same.

In a flash, Susan realized how, over the years, the people around her had poisoned her self-talk, turned her strengths into weaknesses, and made her believe all these negative things about herself. No wonder a stimulating, quick-witted woman with high standards, living in the circumstances she did, was told over and over that she is an aggressive, angry bitch. Sooner or later, we start to believe what people say. But Susan's lights went on that day as we peeled back the layers and revealed her Purpose Statement.

"This is it," Susan said as her truths revealed themselves and the words came to her, "this is how I am. I can't help it. This is me."

Six years later I was giving a keynote speech at The International Plaza Convention Center in Toronto. I'd just got off the escalator when someone called my name.

"Hey, Nick."

I turned.

"You don't remember me do you?" The woman looked familiar.

"Help me out," I said.

"It's me. Susan."

We hugged. "You look wonderful," I said. "What are you doing here?"

"I manage three teams for the Ministry of Agriculture and they're running public focus groups here today," she said giddy with pride. "I'm wandering from room to room keeping an eye on them."

"It's been amazing," she laughed. "Once I realized I was the only one who could change my life, I became really focused and sure of myself. And, believe it or not, I started talking to people I didn't know and one thing led to another.

"Separating what I do—my purpose—from how I do it—my projects—made everything so crystal clear. My Purpose Statement gave me clear guidance, and from that point onward, I just had to ask myself, "Am I doing it now or not?" If I was doing it, I'd feel happy. I began to notice opportunities arising and doors opening, and I acted upon them. It was a bit scary at first."

Susan's Purpose Statement: "I challenge people to imagine wild, new ideas."

How does she do that?

"By producing and managing trade shows for the agricultural sector."

Today, Susan gets paid for doing the things she used to get ridiculed for at home.

In my own life, almost everything I've accomplished began as a 'crazy idea.' Some of them achieved great success, while others faced certain failure.

The defining factor that set them apart was simple: the projects that worked were done for the right reason—purpose. The others may have seemed like a great idea at the time but were done for all the wrong reasons—like chasing easy money or simply seeking temporary amusement.

Until I found my own Purpose Statement when I was fifty-two, no matter what I did, something was always missing. Looking back, I remember spending many hours banished to the corridor at school.

Whenever a teacher said something that had the class looking confused, I'd pipe up and say, "Why don't you just say 'such and such' and we'll all get it?" On one occasion, Mr. Kennedy was trying to explain what the hypotenuse was in the Pythagoras theorem. Everyone was baffled, so I said it was like a ladder leaning against a wall.

"Boothman,! Corridor. I've told you not to do that."

My Purpose Statement? I make complicated concepts sound simple and interesting. How do I do that? By writing books and giving speeches. Today I get paid for doing the things I got punished for at school.

Before I discovered my Purpose Statement, if a friend proposed, "Let's start a fish and chip shop," I might have said, "Sure," without much thought. But now, I can consult my Purpose Statement and confidently say, "Sorry, that's not what I do."

Chapter 23
How You Do It?

Purpose. What you do. Project. How you do it. Different. Distinct. Got it?

For many people, the reason why they work at a job might simply be to pay the bills and have some fun. How they earn that money might be by selling shoes, working at a bank, or cooking in a restaurant. If they don't have a passion for their job, it's a straightforward cause-and-effect transaction: I cook, I get paid. I don't cook, I don't get paid.

However, if you genuinely love selling shoes, working at a bank, or cooking meals and you believe it's your true purpose in life, then it transforms into an enjoyable endeavor that you eagerly jump out of bed for in the morning. And, if you also deeply care about how your job brings magic to the lives of those you serve, that's truly inspiring.

Understanding this separation is empowering. You might pivot, adjust, or evolve your 'how'—the projects, methods, or initiatives—but your core purpose remains constant, providing stability and coherence.

Here are a few more examples of Purpose Statements:

"I search out and bring art to the world."

"I monitor nutrition."

"I challenge the status quo with ideas that are beautiful and user friendly."

"We change the world through stories."

"I give women the courage to succeed."

"I crystalize real good."

"I shepherd lost souls."

"I make learning fun."

See! I'll bet some of these don't mean much to you at all. However "I search out and bring art to the world" does mean the world to Ralph Lauren, the famous American fashion designer. That's what he does.

How does he do it? When he was twenty-six, he was inspired to design a wide, European-style necktie like one he'd seen in a movie. His ideas kept getting rejected, so he started his own company, turning out artistic ties and selling them to small shops in New York City under the name Polo. His purpose? To search out and bring art to the world. Today, Ralph Lauren is a very wealthy man.

"I challenge the status quo with ideas that are beautiful and user friendly," meant the world to Steve Jobs. That's what he did.

How did he do it? By producing computers and phones, and subsequently much more that met his high standards.

"We change the world through stories" does mean the world to the founders of TED talks.

Your Purpose Statement describes WHAT you do, while your project, job, or calling is the HOW you do it. Let's take the example of "I crystalize real good" (his exact words) from the earlier list. These are the words of a talk-show host in Birmingham, Alabama, who had me uncover his Purpose Statement on live radio. As he looked back on his life, he realized he always had a knack for summarizing. So now he can confidently say "I crystallize real good." And when someone asks, "How do you do that?" he can reply, "By interviewing guests and swiftly summarizing what they've said in ways that stick in my audience's minds."

Susan (from the previous story) and I both get paid today for what we used to get into trouble for when we were younger. And we're not alone—many of my workshop students discovered their purpose by examining what they were actually doing when they got into trouble way back when.

Discovering your Purpose Statement starts by getting rid of the clutter you've gathered over the years that's been hiding the true you. The simpler your words, the better. When you watch someone go through this process, you can tell by their face as they get closer. It relaxes them, and they light up inside. Many report that it's like floating. My favorite example of this came in an email after one of my workshops. "I woke up this morning and felt like I'd lost forty pounds."

Everyone has something that comes naturally to them. For some, it's a talent for art or music. For others, it's a knack for problem-solving or athletics. Unfortunately, many people never discover their natural talents because they focus on things that don't come easily to them. If you find yourself struggling to excel in a certain area, it may be time to step back and consider what comes more naturally to you.

You can uncover your own Purpose Statement in the Playbook on page 256.

Chapter 24
Ben's Story

Ben attended one of my workshops. He surprised himself when, eight months later, he said farewell to his career as a financial analyst, raised $300,000 through grants and sponsorships, and opened a high-class bakery staffed, more or less exclusively, by people in their early twenties who'd served time in prison.

A couple of years later, Ben approached me with a request to briefly address one of my workshops. He showed up with an air of sharpness and vigor, his hair cropped close. He looked markedly different from the memory I hold of him—a rotund figure in a loose blue jumper with graying hair.

"Ben?"

"Not bad for a forty-four-year-old ex-tycoon!" he said, beaming.

"Fantastic," is all I managed before he squeezed the life out of me in a bear hug. He introduced himself to the group and then told them this:

"The reason I've come here today is to share with you something I did wrong when I took this workshop. I resisted. When I got the words right, after spending hours asking questions and writing out pages and pages to end up with such an obvious phrase, I actually said out loud to the whole group, 'You mean to say I actually paid money and came all this way to end up with something so trite and simple? I expected more than this; it can't be right.' But I've come to tell you it was right.

"It was simple—so simple, I couldn't believe it. Nick told us all that it could take weeks for what we'd done that day to fully click, for it to go right into our systems and start flowing, and for us to get it. It will come in its own time.

"I left feeling cheated. But less than two weeks later, I woke up in tears. I crept into the bathroom and looked in the mirror, and this voice from inside me just kept whispering, 'Oh my God, oh my God, oh my God.' And I 'got it.' I had my epiphany right there. I cried with happiness. And I couldn't even put into words what I 'got'."

Everyone in the room was staring at Ben. He continued.

"Your Purpose Statement will be simple, it will be obvious, and it will set your spirit free. I also came here to warn you that if you tell your words to anyone else outside of this room before they hit you, you'll dilute their power, and they will seem nothing and trivial. Your Purpose Statement belongs inside you, inside your mind, not outside and spoken; the words are trivial outside of you."

"Once you get it, things start to flow in ways that even Nick's metaphors can't explain. In the beginning, you notice them; after a while, they just become part of your Flowpath."

He paused for so long that a couple of people started clapping. He softly motioned for them to wait.

"Caring and protecting have always been inside me. The difference came when an image of a shepherd flashed across my imagination when I was defining myself. That was the seed that grew into what I do today. My Purpose? I shepherd lost souls. How do I do it? By running a bakery that employs young adults who've served time in prison.

Most of them are touchy-feely, kinesthetic types. They learn and make their decisions based on the way things feel or make them feel. They have a hard time in our visual-based school system. I read how, although we use all our senses to take in the world around us, about half of the population primarily relies on what they see to make sense of the world, they are visual. About one-third rely on touch and physical sensation, they are kinesthetic. The rest rely on the way things sound, they're auditory. The bakery is the perfect kinesthetic place to prepare them to do what comes naturally. It's all hands-on: mixing, kneading, forming, cleaning, teamwork, planning, talking to strangers, and handling money. So that's what I focus on. They learn the literal and spiritual meanings of 'Give us this day our daily bread.'"

Chapter 25
All It Takes Is A Crazy Idea

Everything's been done. Thought. Action. Been there, done that. Right? Wrong. Ideas? From thin air. Twisted. Reframed. Old ideas, new eyes. Innovation? Not dead. Built on the bones of the past. Progress? Recycled genius.

Some of you might already have solid plans for doing your own thing and be well on your way to doing it. However, there are those of you who haven't quite decided yet and are still in the process of searching.

People often say that every possible thought has already been thought of and every possible action has already been taken. While that might be true in a strict sense, it's uplifting to realize that new ideas don't always emerge fully formed out of thin air. More often than not, they are just fresh ways of looking at existing ideas. This doesn't mean that innovation is impossible; rather, it's a reminder that progress is usually built upon what has already been done.

Sometimes, all it takes is a crazy idea. After all, 'crazy's' just another word for passionate, creative, wild, or spontaneous. And 'idea' is another word for purpose, project, or proposal.

Throughout history, we've seen countless crazy ideas that we now accept as common, even though they were mocked at their inception. Back in 1762, John Montagu, the 4th Earl of Sandwich, had a crazy idea. Being a serious gambler, he didn't want to leave the gaming table, even when he got hungry. So he instructed his servants, "Get me some meat between two slices of bread." And that's how the sandwich came about.

Henry Heinz had his own crazy idea: he decided to put tomato ketchup in clear glass bottles so customers could see what they were getting. Levi Strauss had a crazy idea: he fashioned trousers out of tent cloth and reinforced them with rivets. John Kimberly and Charles Clark had a crazy idea: they invented soft tissue paper for removing cold cream. Bill Gates had a crazy idea: to put a computer on every desk.

Today, you can eat a sandwich while you boot up Windows in your Levi's and wipe the ketchup off your fingers with a Kleenex—because these crazy ideas created jobs for countless millions and built considerable fortunes for their originators.

The digital era was shaped by a handful of crazy ideas that changed our lives, like online check depositing, Apple watches, and drones. At first, everyone laughed at them because they seemed ridiculous—until they made them happen, then there was no stopping them. Pop culture is full of stories about people with crazy ideas that turned out to be amazing. Michael Dubin disrupted the shaving world with the Dollar Shave Club, which he sold six years later for one billion dollars. J.K. Rowling went from struggling single mom to the world's most successful author.

In the early days of television, most shows were broadcast live. This meant that if there was a mistake, everyone would see it. So when a young woman named Lucille Ball proposed doing a sitcom that was filmed instead of live, her studio bosses thought she was crazy. But she persisted, and the result was I Love Lucy, one of the most beloved TV shows of all time.

These seemingly wild notions turned out to be strokes of genius, serendipitously transforming industries and everyday life for millions.

Conjure Up A Crazy Idea

Do you have an idea that seems a bit crazy, but you can't quite shake it? Maybe you've been told by others that your idea isn't feasible or won't work. Or maybe you're just not sure if it's the right time to take the plunge. Well, before dismissing your idea entirely, try doing this exercise. You might be surprised at what you find!

- Get a crazy idea, like something from a movie, that needs magic to make it happen.
- Check it aligns with your Purpose Statement.
- Program it into your imagination to make it come alive. Picture it as real; see it, hear it, feel it and, if possible, smell and taste it right there in your imagination.
- Take the first step today.

Picture yourself three months from now, busy making it happen.

Take The First Step

We don't all need crazy ideas but we do all need to take the first step.

Jason is a former lab assistant.

"I was going down the rut route," he told me. "For eleven years, I'd get up at the same time every day, look in the same mirror, drive the same route, see the same faces, and park in the same spot. I remember the day I quit my job. It was a beautiful early summer morning, and as I drove to work, all I could think about was how much I hated it. By the time I got there, I had made up my mind—I was going to quit. I walked into my boss's office and said, 'I'm quitting'. And just like that, with no backup plan or safety net, I started down the path of entrepreneurship. It was one of the craziest things I've ever done, but it also turned out to be one of the best decisions I've ever made."

Jason packed in his well-paid job, sold his house, bought a small farm, and started a business growing herbs and distributing organic seeds online. Today, his wife and oldest son work alongside him full-time. "Going solo was a risk I couldn't afford," he says now, "but I was desperate to be somebody, to leave a legacy. The moment I did it, the next steps were always obvious. I would never have believed how serendipity pulled me along."

Chapter 26
Find Your Flowpath

Your Flowpath is built around your Purpose Statement and is at the very heart of spontaneous success. It is your pure, unadulterated truth. A unique declaration, in just a few catchy words, that embodies your people, your purpose, your project, and your passion. It's like saying to the universe, "Here's exactly who I am and what I stand for, and I trust you to guide me in the best possible way." And then, your subconscious draws on your Primal Powers to orchestrate the alignment of people, events, and circumstances in your favor, almost magically illuminating the path before you.

Let's say I'm on a plane and someone asks, "So, what do you do?"

I say in a super-conversational tone, "You know how some people have trouble connecting and communicating face-to-face?"

"Sure." The person replies. because it's true.

"Well, I write books and give speeches that make it really simple and interesting, so they can meet more people and find fresh opportunities."

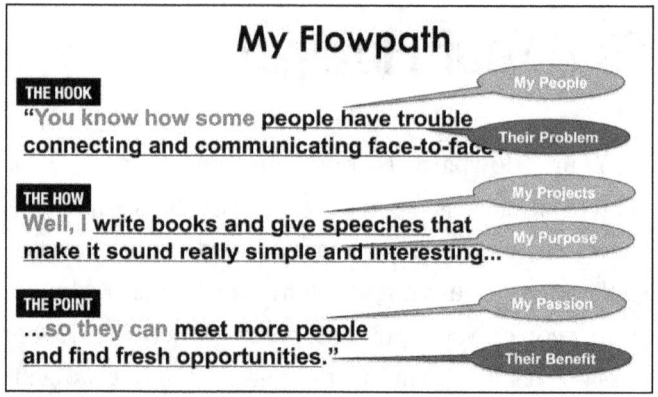

I've just told them what I do, who I do it for, how I do it, what makes my approach different, and what the benefits are to the other person. My people are those who have trouble connecting and communicating face-to-face. Their problem is connecting and communicating face-to-face. My projects: I write books and give speeches. My purpose is to make complicated concepts simple and interesting. My passion: I care deeply about human potential. Their benefit is that they can meet more people and find fresh opportunities.

Presenting this much information in so few words and in a way that an eight-year-old can understand is how you give your passion project "legs." When an idea has legs, it's memorable and easy to spread by word of mouth.

This Flowpath works just as well in a pub as on a plane, at a fund-raiser, or anywhere you're introducing a fresh idea. The trick is to get the other person to say 'yes' before you tell them. Make sure to exclude all jargon and sales pitches and use simple, clear language.

Craft Your Own Flowpath

Answer the following questions, one at a time: Make a note of everything that pops into your mind, then choose the answers that feel the most joyful. This is not fixed in stone. You'll find yourself refining your lists over the next two or three weeks as you test them out. We've covered purpose, projects, and people; now it's up to your Primal Powers to help you craft your first draft of your Flowpath.

Who are the people you want to help? Be specific.

What is their problem? Be specific.

What is your project? Be specific.

What is your Purpose?

What is your passion? Be specific.

What are the benefits you offer them? Be specific.

Once you are certain you have your words, write them on the following blank page.

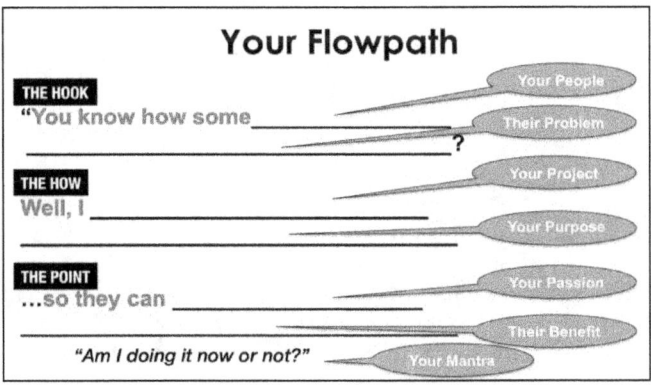

Chapter 27
Talk to a Stranger Today

Life doesn't happen without talking to strangers.
Tim Whyte

Talking to strangers isn't just the right thing to do; it's a matter of survival and a force of nature as old as humanity itself.

Whatever you want in this life—tickets to the World Cup, the perfect partner, or your dream job—chances are you'll need a stranger's help to get it. While strangers hold the keys to much of the joy, knowledge, and hope we experience from day to day, they also hold the keys to something even more exciting: serendipity.

Everyday interactions, like making small talk with the person at the grocery store, "How can I tell if this pineapple is ripe?" At the gym, "Do you prefer cardio or strength training?" In a dog park: "Do you know any good pet-friendly cafes nearby?" Or at a party: "How do you know the host?" can lead to unexpected friendships and lucky breaks. But if you've ever been on the subway or in an elevator, you know the rules. Don't make eye contact, stay as far away from other people as you can, and whatever you do, don't talk to strangers.

But what if the rules are wrong?

Encounters like these happen every day, as long as someone is willing to speak up. Once you make the move and speak up, look for common ground. Common ground is the holy grail of talking to strangers. The moment you find it, you have a bond. The pressure is off, and you can share your stories, your ideas, and your casual chitchat. However, skip the step of finding common ground, and you're playing with fire.

Think of all the people you ignore in a day, a week, or a year. The fellow commuters you never bother talking to, all those people you didn't say hello to at that party last Saturday, the neighbors you never greet, the friendly faces at your place of worship whose eye contact you avoid, the co-workers you see floating around the office and choose to ignore, the three old guys sitting at the table next to you at the café fixing the world's problems.

In my experience, making an instant face-to-face connection with any one of them could have a life-changing impact on your outlook, your confidence, your career, your bottom line, and your lucky breaks. Connecting with the world around you is the right thing to do; but it can be scary.

Talk show hosts, interviewers, and bloggers have a formula for getting people to open up: they start with a statement about the occasion or the location and follow it with an open question. Those are the ones that begin with "who," "where," "why," "when," "what," and "how." On the flight to Las Vegas, Kira, a Canadian, asked Carl, a Norwegian, "Tell me about Oslo. I hear it's a fantastic place (a statement). If I only had four hours, what should I see? (an open question)."

Simple. Now she has him talking. Kira knows the best way to keep him talking is by giving feedback, both physical and verbal. She gives physical feedback by nodding and looking interested, as well as spoken feedback with words like "oh," "aha," and "wow." Kira knows the best open-ended question of all is "Tell me about [insert word here]." And it's not even a question.

Who are these strangers?

Close your eyes and picture some of the strangers you see frequently but never speak to. The ones you sit or stand next to on the bus or train every day or pass by at the office or school. You see them regularly and they see you too. You recognize them; you might even nod or smile or "mouth-Hi" them, but you never actually speak to them. You might walk past a shop every day on the way to work, a shop that you've never been into but you see the shopkeeper every morning, so you smile and nod at each other. We call these people Familiar Strangers.

Perfect Strangers

Perfect Strangers are people you've maybe heard of or read about who you know can help you "perfect" your goals and your dreams. When Elon Musk was in his early twenties, he'd call the Perfect Strangers he'd read about in magazines or seen on TV and ask them out to lunch. Most said no. Some said yes.

Total Strangers

Then there are Total Strangers: people you've never even seen or bumped into yet.

Danger Strangers

These are the people who, right or wrong, set off your fight or flight response the moment you see them. If you've watched enough episodes of Law and Order, seen enough cheesy reality shows, or played enough games of

Grand Theft Auto, you probably have a distorted idea of who you can trust at first sight and who you can't.

Consequential Strangers

"Consequential Strangers" are your neighbors, coworkers, store clerks, local police officers, or members of a religious or community group. They're tradespeople like the butcher, the baker, your mechanic, and the fresh-fruit lady at the market. While we take them for granted, they can enrich our lives in ways we never imagined. Spontaneous Success may most likely come from the word-of-mouth of Consequential Strangers.

Despite the limited connection, they can:
- Offer valuable advice or guidance
- Provide new opportunities or connections
- Challenge your thinking or perspectives
- Support you in times of need
- Inspire or motivate you

These strangers are "consequential" because they can change the course of your life even if you only interact with them briefly.

Chapter 28
One Thing Leads To Another

Thirty years ago, my daughter Kate, who was then 13, came to me one day on the farm and said, "Daddy, they've opened an aromatherapy store in the village; will you drive there so I can see it, please?"

While Kate looked around, I got chatting with Sandy, the owner. She told me she had given up her job in the city to do what she'd always wanted. I told her I was getting out of photography to be a professional speaker because I had met so many people in my travels and in my role as a father who were like roses with rubber bands wrapped around them.

"They'll never blossom until someone removes the metaphorical rubber band to release their potential."

"How?" Sandy asked.

That's when I shared my Flowpath with her.

"You know how some people have trouble connecting and communicating face-to-face?"

"Sure." She nodded.

"Well, I'm writing a book and giving speeches that make it really simple and interesting, so they can meet more people and find fresh opportunities."

Sandy smiled. "I like that."

A few days later, Sandy called to say she's hosting a small gathering at her place to chat about aromatherapy. She asked if I'd come and share what I was doing. I agreed, went over, and spoke for around 20 minutes.

A week later, a woman called and says she was at Sandy's that night, and she has a women's networking group that meets the first Tuesday of every month for lunch. Would I like to come along and talk about what I am doing? I said sure. And I went and spoke.

Two weeks later, a man called and said his cousin was at the women's networking lunch. He asked if I was interested in putting on a workshop for 200 realtors who were in his networking group. I said sure. I put together a workshop, and it was a big success.

Just shy of two months later, I answered the phone, and a woman said, "We are the staging company for AT&T Canada. We heard about what you're doing from someone at a real estate networking workshop. We checked you out and want to invite you to be the opening speaker at the AT&T National Sales Convention at the

Metro Convention Centre in Toronto to address one thousand six hundred people. Are you up for it?"

I said sure. I did it. And it kicked off a chain reaction that lead me to where I am today.

The moral of the story. Never turn down an invitation from your 13-year-old daughter to visit an aromatherapy store that has opened in your local village. Opportunities are everywhere but they rarely knock. You have to get up, get out and talk to strangers.

So, just who are these strangers?

Chapter 29
Street-Smarts and Common Sense

Growing up, I had this friend called Bill. He had this gift that I could only dream of – he could talk to anyone, anywhere, anytime. He could strike up a conversation with a teacher, a shopkeeper, or even a stranger on the street, and somehow, he'd always manage to leave a lasting impression. It was as if he had a magic formula, a secret ingredient that made people want to listen to him, to like him, and to remember him.

As I watched Bill, I'd try and work out how he did it. Was it the way he listened intently to others, making them feel heard and understood? Was it the way he told stories, weaving intricate tales that captivated his audience? Or was it just the way he stood, or sat?

Whatever it was, I knew I wanted some of it. I wanted to be like Bill—a right little charmer.

But, it doesn't work that way.

If the thought of talking to strangers is difficult, try small talk instead. Talking is often serious, structured, and scary; small talk is short and trivial, and nobody notices if you mess up.

Small Talk Isn't Meant to be a Struggle

Small talk is just casual chat about nothing in particular in order to find common ground.

In spite of seeming to have little useful purpose, small talk is a bonding ritual and a strategy for quickly building trust, finding common ground, sensing energy levels and managing interpersonal distance. Small talk helps define relationships between friends, work colleagues, and new acquaintances by quickly exploring and defining each other's social position. Most importantly it allows people to signal their mood, sense the mood of the other person and determine the next move.

Ask questions about what he or she likes to do in their spare time. Where are you from/going? Family? Fun? Current affairs: the weather, the news, sports will do in a pinch. Or your community or a new restaurant nearby. You can natter about pop culture: ask about social media, music, or TV shows. Talk about movies you've just seen or music you've just heard. Or Martin Scorsese, or So you think you can dance, or Dog

Whispering. Or mention a new band or the latest bestselling book. You could remark on a piece of clothing or accessory. An easy and natural comment about the occasion or location followed by an open question works wonders. You don't need to agonize over sparkling opening lines just say something then add a tag question (isn't it? don't they? doesn't it?) You can complement (only if you mean it) something they're wearing or an accessory. Ask where it came from.

Start simple and safe. Chat with the stranger who lives next door. Chat with the checkout guy at the supermarket; chat with the server at the coffee shop. Chat with everyone. Chat, fail, then chat again. Fail and fail again, and brush yourself off and chat again. Because maybe, just maybe, in those chats, you'll find a connection you never expected. Maybe you'll stumble upon an opportunity that changes your life. Maybe you'll discover a new friend or mentor. But you'll never know unless you keep on chatting, keep on learning, and keep on growing. Believe in the power of connection to light up new Flowpaths and forge unexpected bonds. Who knows what incredible adventures await when you dare to engage with the world around you? Who knows what messages of wisdom, kindness, or inspiration you might deliver to others with just a simple conversation?

The world isn't a TV show or a video game; it's a real reality. Your street smarts and common sense should tell you not to walk alone down dark alleys at night, not to flash wads of cash in public, and not to get drunk in places you don't know.

It has never been more important to talk to strangers than it is today. Polarized politics, political correctness, and digital distractions are pushing us apart and making strangers out of all of us. The result is an epidemic of anxiety, isolation, and loneliness across all age, workplace, cultural, and socio-economic groups.

But it doesn't have to be that way.

Chapter 30
A Nod From The Universe

It was a crisp March morning in New York City, the kind of day that makes you feel alive. It was 2008, and I was on the last day of a grueling twenty-city tour, promoting my latest book. I was feeling a mix of emotions - exhaustion, relief, and a hint of uncertainty.

As I strolled down Fifth Avenue, I couldn't help but wonder how my book would be received. Would it resonate with people, or would it fall flat? I longed for a sign, a nod from the universe that the two years I'd spent researching and writing were worthwhile.

The book opens with a quote by Luciano De Crescenzo, a famous Italian writer and director: "We are each of us angels with only one wing, and we can only fly by embracing one another." The word angel comes from the Greek word 'angelos', meaning messenger.

Feeling the need to sit quietly and reflect, I

noticed Saint Patrick's Cathedral at Fifth and Fifty-First. Its Gothic spires and stunning stained-glass windows beckoned me to enter. However, as soon as I walked in, a voice in my head said, 'No, not here. This is not for you.' The words were clear and unmistakable, and I felt a familiar shiver run down my spine.

I turned around and left, the familiar chill of loss settling deep. Forty-seven years. That's how long I'd thought I'd buried it. The raw, echoing pain of that day in another church. I'd convinced myself I'd moved on, healed. But standing there, in the shadow of Saint Patrick's soaring arches, it all came flooding back. Was it the echoing space, the stained light, some faint, lingering echo of the past? I didn't know. All I knew was that my body remembered, even if my mind had tried to forget. And it was screaming, 'Get out.' But even as that primal urge drove me away, another, stronger force, a pull I couldn't explain, drew me further up Fifth Avenue. Three blocks later, when I stepped through the doors of Saint Thomas Church, the chaos inside me stilled. A profound peace settled, a stark contrast to the fear I'd just fled."

"Where shall I sit?" I whispered to myself. 'I know. I'm sixty-two. I'll sit in pew sixty-two'. I walked down the center aisle and found it. The church was empty. I went about ten feet in and sat down.

After fifteen minutes of quiet contemplation, seeking inspiration for my next book, I randomly grabbed a prayer book from the rack in front of me and started flipping through the pages. I wasn't looking for anything in particular, just browsing. And then, something inside the back cover caught my eye. There, handwritten in Portuguese, my second language, was a quote that made my heart skip a beat: "We are each of us angels with only one wing, and we can only fly by embracing one another."

I couldn't believe it. It was like the universe was sending me a message. "No one's going to believe this," I thought to myself, so I pulled out my BlackBerry and took a picture of it. I wanted proof that this was real.

But that was just the beginning.

Chapter 31
A Confession

I'd no sooner taken the photo when I heard the click-clack of a woman's shoes coming up behind me. They stopped several rows back, and all went quiet. I was still holding the prayer book when they started up again. Then a woman slid in beside me. A whispered "Hello, Mister Nick" sent shivers down my spine.

As I turned to face the voice, my eyes met the striking features of someone I vaguely recognized. Her stylish attire and striking features seemed out of place in the quiet church.

"Francesca?"

It must be 40 years. Now, I was in double shock.

"It's an unbelievable coincidence," she whispered, her hand on my arm. "My mother called me to find you just last night, and then I saw you on TV this morning."

I was speechless.

She paused, her expression turning serious. "I live in New York now; I work for the UN. But something bad has happened. My mother told me that Tomaz was in an accident - he fell out of a hot air balloon. She urged me to find you and break the news."

"What's going on? You said Thomas was in an accident... is he okay?"

"I'll tell you everything, but please, come with me,"

"No, tell me now. Is he... alive?"

She hesitated, then nodded. "Yes, he's alive. But we need to go. Now."

Francesca took my hand, her expression somber. "Come with me," she said, leading me out of the cathedral towards a waiting limousine.

As we glided away from the curb, I asked, "How did you find me?"

"Your publisher gave me your handler's number," she replied, her eyes locked on mine. "I saw you leave St. Patrick's and followed you."

Francesca's urgency was palpable. "I'm flying to Faro tonight. You can come." I hesitated, torn between my original plan and the weight of our shared past. But I owed Thomas too much. My mind raced with resistance – all the reasons I shouldn't drop everything and follow her. What about my commitments? The deadlines looming? The carefully laid plans? My family?

But then I heard Thomas's voice in my mind. His wisdom, his guidance, and his unwavering support. I owed him too much to ignore the synchronicity of this moment.

"I have to make a couple of calls, but yes. Okay."

As the limo sped off, I felt the threads of fate weaving together, drawing me into a new adventure. The coincidence of our meeting in Saint Thomas Church of all places seemed more than just chance; it was a sign that our paths were to cross again. The unknown beckoned, and I was powerless to resist.

Over the next few hours, I cut short my last day on tour, got Wendy's blessing and learned that a diplomatic passport can move mountains. Little Francesca Viera, now the Unit Chief in the Portuguese Department of Global Communications at the United Nations Headquarters, could pull a lot of strings, including last-minute business-class seats for two to Faro on TAP, the Portuguese national airline.

Over dinner at 37,000 feet, we caught up.

Francesca was obviously happy for us to be together, but her nervous body language and lack of eye contact were sending mixed messages. After dinner, she ordered a Macieira brandy for each of us. Then another. Then, reaching into her handbag, she nervously pulled out a small photo album.

"Mister Nick, I have a confession to make." She opened the album.

"Ok," I interrupted, "and I have a favor to ask."

She took a healthy swig of the Macieira. So did I. "Cheers."

"Please, Francesca, don't call me Mister Nick anymore. Just Nick, or even Nicko, but forget the 'Mister'."

"Ha! On one condition then. I'm Frankie." No longer nervous, she laughed. "Ok Nicko, cheers."

We clinked our brandy snifters.

"Cheers, Frankie."

She hit the call button and ordered two more Macieiras."

"Now. About this confession."

"I want you to see something," she said, flipping the pages of the photo album slowly.

First were some snaps of Lavanda. It had changed and she had to explain where things were. Then came a few snaps of Casilda in a real estate office. She stopped at a snapshot of Thomas waving from the Oldsmobile and flattened the album out. With him was a young girl in the passenger seat. Francesca pointed to the girl.

"Do you remember the night before you left Lavanda?

"That was a very emotional night for me."

"This girl," she said, pointing to the girl in the car. "She delivered an envelope to you."

"A child in a Benfica shirt?"

"This is Lara. Tomaz's daughter. That envelope ended up in the garbage, covered in mustard. I rescued it. I opened it, and cleaned it, and put it in a fresh envelope from the store." She blushed, and her chin trembled. "But I read it. I am sorry, and I'm ashamed. I know better."

As we soared through the night sky, from New York to Faro the cabin lights dimmed. I reached out and gently placed my hand on hers. She gave a tight smile and shook her head, her eyes glinting with a mix of emotions.

"At first, it seemed so... insignificant, so fleeting," she began, her voice barely above a whisper. "But I don't know... For me, was it a sign, a message from God? Or was it just rubbish, the ramblings of a crazy old man?" She paused, her gaze drifting off into the distance. "But Tomaz is not crazy."

I felt a shiver run down my spine as she turned her attention back to me, her eyes locking onto mine with an intensity that made my heart skip a beat.

"I had to get it to you, so I memorized it in English," she said, her voice filled with a sense of urgency. And then, in a tone that was both reverent and awe-inspired, she spoke the words that would change everything:

"Navigate the currents of life with grace and resilience; embrace the unknown with open arms, for there is magic in the unknown."

She paused, taking a deep breath as if to calm the storm brewing inside her.

"Find beauty and meaning in the simplest of moments, and know that each circumstance that comes your way is part of a perfect plan to transform your purpose into tangible reality."

"Tears of joy," she said, wiping her eyes. She loosened her seatbelt and turned to me.

"I had forced my feelings away my whole life. Suddenly, I noticed things I'd never seen before. And then, one morning, like a flash of lightning, I saw Hazel on the Fisherman's Beach.

"I walked towards her, feeling a strange pull. She was alone, and I knew in that instant that I had to talk to her. She was on vacation from Zurich. She was a teacher at a fancy girls' school. It was love at first sight, right there. Little did I know that that chance encounter would lead me to Zurich, to a new life, and to a love that would transform me forever.

"The words in the letter were so irresistible I wrote them down for my mother and she memorized them too. And today she's a big shot in real estate."

Francesca's eyes shone with purpose as she continued, "Finding Hazel was just the beginning. I realized I'd been living my family's dream, suppressing my own desires and passions. But Hazel's love and support gave me the courage to explore my own interests and talents."

She paused, a determined look on her face. "Living in Lavanda with all the tourists, and speaking the English you taught me, I discovered a passion for bringing different types of people together and getting them to understand each other. In Zurich I got a job as a translator at the United Nations. From there it was just one great thing leading to another.

"Today, I use my skills to amplify the voices of those who need to be heard."

"Whatever happened to her? Thomas's daughter."

"She married a sculptor called Declan, Declan Quinn and they moved to Ireland. She was pregnant when

Declan was killed by accident in a police chase. Tragic, especially when you consider everything else. She went back to Lavanda with her little boy. She has many friends and a lot of support there, and she's made quite a name for herself."

The next morning, as the Boeing 767 prepared to land, the pristine golden beaches and glistening turquoise water of the Algarve coast gave way to sparkling high-rise buildings on the Faro coast. As we stepped out onto the gangway ladder, the hot air and the rich aroma of coffee and charcoal-grilled sardines left no doubt as to where we were.

Donna Casilda was there to meet us.

Chapter 32
Diva Ceramica

We sped through crowded streets in her fancy Mercedes-Benz 500, eventually arriving at the cliff road. The once sleepy fishing village of Praia de Lavanda was now a vibrant global destination, transformed by an influx of over ten million visitors annually.

As we roared past five-star hotels, restaurants, and shops, we swung south to the lighthouse, where a gallery stood in place of the old lighthouse keeper's cottage. The Take Five Gallery sign above the plate glass window confirmed we had arrived.

"Go ahead," Casilda said, as I stepped out of the car and she took Francesca's arm. "We'll be there in a minute."

Inside, the ceramics gallery was a sensory feast - a kaleidoscope of colors, textures, and shapes. A signature across the back wall read "Lara Quinn, Diva Ceramica."

A woman emerged from behind a vibrant, floral-patterned panel, her brightly colored suit a mesmerizing blend of turquoise, yellow, and orange, perfectly suited to the lively atmosphere

I said hello.

"Hello," she replied, her voice warm and sweet. "I believe you're here to see my father."

We shook hands, and I asked pointing to the signature on the wall. "You're that Lara?"

"I am."

Memories came rushing back. "You made me cry," I said, exhaling deeply.

She leaned in, her voice barely above a whisper. "I brought you a message the night Benfica won... and you lost it." A hint of a smile played on her lips.

I marveled at her remembering our encounter from so long ago. "You were six?" I asked, impressed, my eyes widening slightly as I recalculated the years, astonished by her remarkable recall.

Her smile blossomed, and she nodded, seeming to relish the surprise she'd sparked.

A young man in his early twenties in a Take Five T-shirt and chinos appeared from behind another panel pushing a wheelchair. In it was a tall, skinny man wearing a richly embroidered Middle Eastern hat.

"Nicko, my boy. Splendid to see you. Sorry, I can't get up." It was Thomas. He looked old but sounded as radiant as ever.

"Jeepers, I thought you were dying," I said.

"So did I. Fell out of a hot air balloon!"

He still had his larger-than-life, rich theatrical delivery.

"Grandpa, it was on the ground."

"What!" I said laughing. "How do you even do that?"

"Grounded for life." Thomas retorted.

The young man laughed along and introduced himself. "Hello, I'm Paul."

Casilda and Frankie burst in with a flurry of curiosity.

"Good God in heaven," Thomas brayed. "Francesca, whoops, Frankie, is that you? You look bloody marvelous."

"Mum," Paul said, "Frankie's cut her hair short and gelled it back. Looks awesome. And her clothes are trim and tailored."

"How exciting. Frankie, come, come." She went over to Lara arms outstretched and they hugged. Oh, my goodness, it's been so long," Lara said.

Lara ran her hand down Frankie's lapel.

"Oh, this is lovely. Linen?" Lara asked. "What color is it?" And, as Lara rubbed the fabric between her fingers, I got the shock of my life.

She's blind! Lara is blind!

Surprise, confusion, disbelief? What was I feeling?

"Green. Pale green." Frankie replied.

"Nicko, what's up?" Thomas bellowed. He could see the shock on my face and the reason why.

"I never mentioned it before?" he asked.

I shook my head.

Lara turned to me with a calm voice and a slight smile, evidently already aware of my realization.

"Didn't you know I can't see?"

Despite the awkwardness, I could tell from her expression that she accepted my ignorance without criticism.

"It's okay," she said calmly. "I'm used to having conversations like this."

I was speechless.

"Don't get fooled by appearances. I can pick up on your emotions and your intentions; right now, I sense your confusion."

Paul was grinning; he'd heard it all before. Frankie stepped away from Casilda and Thomas got up out of the wheelchair. "Hell, these things are uncomfortable! I can't keep this charade up any longer. I'm as fit as a bloody fiddle."

Just yesterday, I'd been sitting in the quiet sanctuary of a Manhattan church, and now, twenty-four hours later, I was back in the chaotic land of sudden, unpredictable surprises, the kind I secretly thrived on, and I couldn't help but wonder, with a rising sense of anticipation, what shocking twist would unfold next, a wave of intense shock, relief, and gratitude washing over me in a confusing, exhilarating rush.

"What's going on?" Frankie demanded. "I'm sorry, Nicko; Tomaz is clearly not dying. Why all the drama to get us here?"

Casilda stepped forward. "Perhaps we should all sit down."

With a gentle pause, she waited for the room to quiet, her eyes locking onto the faces before her. Paul switched the open sign to closed. Then, in a voice filled with conviction and emotion, she began to speak in English.

"I know what it's like to feel trapped in a cycle of struggle. I was once a poor woman, desperate to make ends meet, to provide for my loved ones. The weight of responsibility was crushing at times. I never had the privilege of college, so I took on any job that came my way, no matter how tough. But despite the hardships, a fire burned within me - a fierce ambition, a longing to break free and make a meaningful mark on this world. I dreamed of doing something extraordinary, something that would bring hope and light to others."

Her voice trembled with emotion as she continued, "Ten days ago, I stood at the beginning of a new journey. I closed the largest real estate deal of my life, a moment of joy that gave value to my struggles. And as I watched almost sixteen million euros flow into my bank account, I felt an overwhelming sense of pride, vindication, and gratitude. Tears of joy streamed down my face as I thought of the long, arduous path that led me here - the sleepless nights, the setbacks, the doubters. But most of all, I thought of my family, and those whose support and love fueled my determination to succeed."

I felt the breath go out of everyone around me. Everyone except Paul. He stood there with a serene smile on his face. After all, it turns out that he masterminded Casilda's two successful land-banking projects over the past three years—one for the hotel that had just made her a fortune and the other for her passion project.

I learned later that after Francesca left and Casilda's husband passed away, she took on Paul as an office boy. He filled the gap in her heart. She enrolled him in a six-week business essentials program in Lisbon. While he was there, he met Veronika, a young Croatian woman who'd been working as a set designer at the campus theater. He persuaded her to become the chief colorist in charge of the hand painters at the gallery.

It took a while for the congratulations and cheers to settle down, then Casilda continued.

"I was surprised by the turn of events, so I dug deeper. It started at the Hole in the Wall, where Nicko taught me English. That's where my new life began. I loved learning and teaching together.

"Then, a German woman tried to buy the barber shop up the street to open a real-estate office and I felt angry. I realized the locals would be forced out because they couldn't afford to live here anymore. So I got my real estate license and was successful from the start. What I knew, and what the foreign realtors didn't know, was that many of the properties and houses around Lavanda weren't owned by just one person. A son might own the rights to a bedroom, the mother to the kitchen and the grandfather to the garden. They'd been bequeathed for generations, so an outside developer would never get them all to agree to sell. But I could. I was trusted. I did the best for them.

"As our village prospered, I watched friends and neighbors sell their homes, only to be priced out of the market. They struggled to find new roots, while I prospered. The guilt gnawed at me, seeing loved ones forced to leave, their connections severed. That's when I had a crazy idea took.

"I've always had a gift for making strangers feel like family. And I wanted to bring home those who truly belonged here.

"With Paul's support, we crafted a dream project – Lavender Valley. A haven for those born and raised here, who yearn to grow old in the only home they've ever known.

"Tomorrow, we break ground on this labor of love. Francesca, Nicko, please forgive the dramatic invitation, but I needed you to be here.

"Actually, that was my bright idea," Thomas interrupted. "Not my finest moment. Nevertheless, it's true. I was trying to capture a photo of the balloon firing the burner for take-off. I was inside the basket leaning back, looking up, and then I just flipped out—backwards, like a clown at a children's party. Not exactly a dignified exit."

Casilda continued. "I only got final permission three days ago. Your presence, along with Tomaz and Paul, means everything to me. Lavender Valley is more than just a project - it's about people. We've reserved homes for displaced community members to return and live affordably, with minimal rent—where they belong. When they pass, the homes will return to the company, ensuring the legacy continues."

Lara stood up. Watching her body language, I felt that she was hiding an inner pain behind her smile. I sensed that though she had contributed significantly to Paul and Casilda's project, she felt hurt and frustrated at being overlooked. She resented being treated with less respect than others.

Now it was my turn.

"May I say a few words?"

I waited for Lara and Casilda to sit.

"Dear Casilda, your project is amazing, and your heart is kind and generous. But perhaps you've overlooked the most important part of your journey - the Messenger who delivered a life-changing letter to me at the perfect moment.

"Lara, you played a crucial role in this chain reaction, and your timing has impacted millions. Your actions influenced my writing, which in turn inspired others, and will soon impact the lives of those who will live in Casilda's new homes. You can't deny the ripple effect of your actions. God bless you for being the messenger of serendipity.

Thomas took Lara's hand. "He's right, you know. Bloody perfect every time."

"Thank you for your kind words, Nicko," Thomas began. "And while it is natural to believe that the message itself is more important than how it is delivered, the power of a message delivered by a child is undeniable. The physical exchange between generations from one hand to another proves more than words could ever express. So yes, my darling Lara, the part you played is one of immense value."

Lara's face lit up with a radiant smile, her eyebrows rising slightly as she listened to the heartfelt words. Her ears, attuned to the nuances of sound, drank in the praise, and her head nodded subtly, as if savoring each phrase.

"Thanks Dad," she whispered, her voice trembling, as she turned to me. "And thank you, Nicko, for understanding."

Lara's smile remained, her cheeks flushed with pleasure, as she absorbed the significance of her actions. Her posture straightened, conveying a sense of pride and accomplishment, her other senses heightened as she basked in the warmth of the moment.

Chapter 33
A Journal

Paul had been quietly listening, waiting for the right moment to speak up.

" Grandpa, Mum showed me your journal."

"Paul!" Lara snapped.

"That's perfectly fine, my dear. I gave it to you for safekeeping. It's just stories from my past, notes from my journalism days… and some life lessons learned along the way. I thought it might be time one day soon to pass on some family history. I'm delighted that Paul's interested."

Thomas was sitting on the edge of the table, breathing slowly. "Go ahead, my boy."

Paul's curiosity spilled over. "It's filled with strange symbols and mystical words. I thought it was an ancient language or a secret code. Mom asked me to read it to her, but I couldn't make sense of it, so instead, I promised her that one day I'd ask you to tell us how you became so smart."

Thomas laughed. "Smart? Me? I'm not smart; I just...Okay, fine. Maybe I've learned a thing or two. But most of what I learned was too complicated for me to remember, which is why I wrote it all down.

"Come on, Thomas!" I joined in. "You're always saying profound stuff and knowing exactly what to do. How did you get so wise?"

"I'm not wise! I've just lived a long life, and I've made a lot of mistakes. I learned to embrace simplicity and let go of complexity."

"But Grandpa, you're always telling us to embrace the unknown and share our stories. Isn't it time you practiced what you preach?"

Thomas chuckled. "I hope I don't preach. Here, hand me that."

Paul passed the journal to Thomas.

"Well, my boy," he began, his voice low and soothing, "I'll do my best to keep it short and sweet." As he flipped through the pages, his eyes scanned the notes, his expression softening. Pausing, he stroked a page with a nostalgic smile, then rose from his seat, his eyes sparkling with memories."

"It was 1959, and I was 23. I was making a bit of a name for myself as a crime reporter in London. Then, one day, I got an assignment to report on the Chinese famine from the Walled City of Kowloon, British Hong Kong's most notorious district. They called it the City of Darkness; it was the most densely crowded place on earth and the home of the local triad gangs."

"Wow, Thomas," Frankie interrupted. "It sounds terrifying?"

"Indeed it was. Early one morning, I'm in a teashop, making notes, in shorthand, and minding my own business when the security police grabbed me, confiscated this very journal, carted me off, and accused me of being a spy."

"What's shorthand?" Paul asked.

Thomas leaned forward, a hint of nostalgia in his eyes. He turned the book to face Paul and pointed to the page. "This is."

"Back in my journalism days, we didn't have recorders or smartphones. Shorthand was our go-to trick for taking notes and capturing quotes. But the Hong Kong authorities thought I was using some secret spy language. Sound familiar?

Paul nodded and shrugged.

"I couldn't believe what was happening. I'd just been enjoying a cup of Jasmine tea and, well, asking a few questions."

"And did they buy it?" Paul replied.

"The next few days were a blur of darkness and indignity. Locked in a filthy cramped cell and dragged off to endless interrogations. But I didn't lose it. My spirit remained intact.

Thomas paused, his eyes distant, lost in the memory. What happened next? How did he escape? The questions hung in the air.

Chapter 34
A Holy Man

"It was there, in that rat infested hole, that I met a holy man. His name was Raghu. Clad in a long brown woolen cloak with a hood, there was something otherworldly about him. The cell was dingy and grim, but despite the bleak surroundings, there was something 'delightful' about the figure before me. I'm usually never at a loss for words, but this man left me speechless."

"A holy man in the City of Darkness?" Casilda said. Why did you trust him, Thomas? Was it his words, or some kind of feeling?"

"He'd scratched five simple words in English on the cell wall: 'Stop looking and start seeing.' Those words eventually became my mantra, guiding me through the darkness and shaping the rest of my adventures.

"He said, 'Life's not about finding your future; it's about your future finding you,' and he really got me thinking. It's like, instead of always chasing after what we think we want, we need to stop, open our eyes, and pay attention to what's trying to find us.

Paul, his young mind buzzing with curiosity, couldn't contain himself. "How, Grandpa? What did he do?"

"On the third day, he was just sitting there when something bizarre happened—a new guard, someone who hadn't been there before, asked Raghu about the words on the wall."

Thomas leaned in, his voice softening. "This guard ended up connecting Raghu with a lawyer and within two days, the lawyer took on the case at no cost, got all charges dropped against him, and set him free. Just like that, he was gone. As far as I knew, Raghu hadn't done anything special. It just all seemed so natural, like the universe had arranged the whole thing."

Frankie raised an eyebrow. "Sounds too good to be true if you ask me."

Paul nodded in agreement. "He must've had some connections."

Casilda's eyes sparkled. "Well, I think it's amazing! Like a miracle."

"He called it a Flowpath, a sweet spot where purpose, people, passion, and projects align in their own time. I would never have believed it but his release from jail was utterly bewildering. Then I was released the same day. Mistaken identity!

"Perhaps Raghu's experience teaches us to trust in the unknown." Lara said. "Two releases in one day from a place like that? That's mind-blowing!"

"Yes it is. In that unlikely place, Raghu showed me the power of living spontaneously and embracing the unknown. He'd unlocked a door within me to a world where even captivity could not confine my spirit."

Frankie leaned in, her voice filled with interest, "Did you stay in touch?"

"I couldn't get Raghu out of my head. I had to find out what happened to him. I used my journalism connections and tracked him down to a monastery in Macau, on the Sai Van River. I gave up my job and determined to track him down. I was hungry for more"

Lara thought aloud, "Do you think Raghu's experience totally changed his life?"

"I actually found out it did," Thomas replied. "He was the Abbot now."

"As I entered the monastery courtyard, Raghu emerged from the shadows, his eyes still twinkling with warmth. He opened his arms, and I felt the same sense of calm wash over me. Gone was the brown woolen cloak. In its place, a simple elegant celestial blue robe tied with a narrow golden silk sash that seemed to blend into the misty mountainside. On his feet he wore woven straw sandals, secured with simple leather straps."

"'You have come home,' he said, his voice gentle as the breeze. He invited me to stay and I accepted."

Thomas paused, the memory of that moment hanging in the air. What happened next? What did he learn from Raghu? The questions burned in their eyes, eager for the next chapter of the story.

Thomas dragged a folding chair across the floor. He positioned it directly in front of us, his eyes locking onto each of ours in turn. His eyes softened, and his breath caught. Memories, long buried, began to resurface. His gaze drifted inward, and for an instant, he was lost in the depths of his own soul.

"For one year," he whispered, his voice barely audible, "I immersed myself in the monastery's rhythms. I woke with the sun, and slept with the stars. I learned to speak Portuguese. I worked in the monastery's gardens, nurturing life from the earth, and watching the seasons unfold." His hands appeared to move spontaneously, as though he was grasping an unseen matrix. "And I restored ancient documents, piecing together fragments of forgotten knowledge."

Frankie's eyes widened, her voice filled with awe, "You found a whole new world."

Lara leaned in, her curiosity piqued, "And what did you discover about yourself?"

Paul's brow furrowed, his tone skeptical, "Timeless moment? What do you mean?"

"After supper, Raghu and I would sit on the rooftop, watching the stars and sharing our discoveries—and occasionally, our shared love of jazz.

Joyful to talk in his native language, Raghu revealed an uncanny connection he'd uncovered between faith and fortune while listening to Dave Brubeck's iconic recording of Take Five.

"This is awesome," Paul remarked, his eyes wide with fascination. Thomas continued, referring to his journal from time to time.

"Here," he said, and he read.

"Raghu insisted that tune has a deeper connection to the universe than we realize. It's not just the music—it's written in 5/4 time. Some experts believe the addictive drum pattern was inspired by Indian rhythms; others, that it was Bulgarian street musicians in Turkey; either way, it got him thinking."

Thomas paused, flipping through the dog-eared pages. "Here," he said, and he read. "The 5/4 rhythm resonates with the fundamental patterns of nature—the five elements, the five senses, the five points of the star. It's as if Brubeck tapped into the underlying harmony of the universe."

I was starting to grasp his meaning.

"Raghu described something called the Fibonacci sequence—1, 1, 2, 3, 5... The proportions of the universe, from the arrangement of leaves on a stem to the spirals of galaxies, are all rooted in this sequence. Take Five's rhythm echoes this sacred geometry."

Paul leaned forward, fascinated. "You're saying the music is a reflection of the cosmic order?"

"It's a quantum layer where ideas behave in ways that are quite different from what we experience in our everyday world. He talked of something he called retrocausality: when the future affects the past. Where the effect changes the cause. How he came to this point is as fascinating as it is mind-bending science with the potential—if proven true—to alter everything we understand of the world.

"Think about it: Jesus, Mohammed, Abraham, Lao Tzu, Buddha and all the great prophets—all these figures stepped outside the known, the certain. They embraced the vast unknown, the uncertainty of faith. They didn't have a step-by-step plan, a guaranteed outcome. They listened to a voice within, a calling that led them into the wilderness, into the heart of uncertainty. And it was in that uncertainty, in that surrender to something beyond themselves, that they found their power.

"Their messages, their teachings, their very existence – they ripple through time, shaping our world even today. It's like their future impact, the faith they inspired, somehow echoed back to influence their actions, their choices, their destinies. It's a kind of retrocausality, a future shaping the past. And it's a testament to the power of uncertainty, the potential that lies dormant within the unknown. They didn't cling to the familiar, the safe, the predictable. They embraced the void, the mystery, the doubt. And in doing so, they became conduits for something far greater than themselves, something that continues to resonate across centuries and cultures.

"When we let go of the need to control, to predict, to know, we open ourselves up to the infinite possibilities that lie dormant within the field of uncertainty. We become vessels for something greater than ourselves, conduits for a future that is yearning to be born. And that, is the essence of spontaneous success – allowing the future to pull us forward, to shape our present, to guide us towards a destiny that is both unexpected and inevitable.

"Raghu insisted that in this realm, the laws of classical physics that we are familiar with do not apply, and chance encounters and happy accidents appear as our thoughts expand."

"The Flowpath is an expression of oneness." I piped up unable to stay quiet any longer. "It doesn't care about your wants; it only cares about your needs. The secret to the Flowpath is being able to turn what you want into what you need. But there's a catch; it's not just about personal gain; it's about creating something that benefits others. When we align with this harmony, events unfold effortlessly. What we need emerges naturally, and we're guided toward our highest good—and the good of those around us."

Thomas extended his arms to us.

" Yes Nicko. This is the common thread that unites the scriptures and the quantum."

"It's beautiful," Frankie said her voice barely above a whisper.

"And it's always available to those who have eyes to see." Thomas said standing up. "Perhaps, those who see with their hearts, like Lara, are the ones who truly understand the harmony that underlies all things.

"As the nights blended together and Raghu's wisdom seeped into my soul, our conversations reached their natural crescendo. It was time for me to begin my journey home, carrying the embers of our shared insights to illuminate my own path.

"I bade farewell to my friend and began the long journey from Macau to England, visiting holy sites along the way. But my journey took an unexpected turn. And so...I arrived here in Lavanda eight months later through pure serendipity—what else? I was on my way from Marrakesh to Fatima, and I turned south by mistake when I should have kept going. The fragrance of lavender and the laid-back, bohemian atmosphere of this village were exactly what I had been looking for, and I knew that this was where my path had been leading me all along."

Casilda chuckled, her eyes twinkling, "Only you, Thomas, could find paradise by mistake."

"You're not going to tell us you had a vision, are you?" Frankie teased.

"What made you certain this was the place, Dad?"

"You've found your haven, Thomas." I said. "You deserve it."

Thomas stood up and came over to me. "Nicko, my old friend, it's been far too long." The simplicity of his words belied the depth of feeling behind them.

Paul wrapped his arm tenderly around his mother's shoulder, while Frankie and Casilda intertwined their fingers, radiating joy."

Embracing the unknown invites serendipity to flourish. As people, purpose, projects, and passion align, probability fields shift. The result? A Flowpath where success unfolds unexpectedly, and needs are met. Coincidence transforms into synchronicity and the universe whispers, 'You're on the right path.'"

Thomas chuckled and shrugged. "And you know what I figured out after all this wandering and wondering?

"All these stories, these adventures, and the achievements—they're all just different ways of saying, 'Hey, you can do it too!'"

There was a rap on the front door. Paul went over to see who it was.

"Tourists!" He exclaimed. "Two coach-loads."

I stood there smiling, marveling at the mystery of it all.

SPONTANEOUS SUCCESS

NICHOLAS BOOTHMAN

The Spontaneous Success Playbook

Create Your Purpose Statement

To get started, make a list of the things you enjoy doing most. What are you drawn to? What do you find yourself doing even when you don't have to? When do you find yourself losing track of time when you're engaged in an activity? It's probably something that comes naturally to you. If you love spending time outdoors, jot that down. Or, if you enjoy helping others, make a note of that. What have you always been good at? What are your strengths? What do people always come to you for help with? If you're good at problem solving or public speaking, write them down too.

Outside of your family and friends, who in the world do you care about most? Which segments of society deserve to benefit from your time and talents? List seven and prioritize them to three. These are all clues that can help you reveal your birthright.

Next, make a list of all the topics you're passionate about. These can be big or small, from your family to your hobbies to your work. Once you have your list, ask yourself how you could bring a fresh approach to this topic. For example, if you're passionate about art and gardening, you could develop a fresh approach to landscaping. Or if you're passionate about justice but can't abide arguing, you could become a speaker with a fresh approach to conflict resolution.

It is often said that there is nothing new under the sun. But while it may be true that all the basic ideas have been explored, there are still endless possibilities for how those ideas can be combined and applied. In any field, it is always possible to find new ways of looking at old problems. This is especially true when it comes to doing your thing. When we embark on a new project or venture, we have the opportunity to approach it with a fresh perspective. We can look at the situation with new eyes and see things that we didn't notice before. And by bringing a fresh approach to a popular topic, we can breathe new life into it and find solutions that were previously hidden.

Aim for as few words as possible. Four to eight is enough. "I make learning fun." "I connect people and ideas." "I give women the courage to succeed."

Finding your "perfect verb" is the first milestone. You'll find it lurking somewhere, just below the surface of your talents. As you stare at the list, something beckons you. Something is taking shape; something feels good in your body, and it feels right. Let your subconscious help you.

From your notes, find a group of people that you care about or are drawn to—your intended beneficiary. The more specific the group, the better.

Armed with your perfect verb and a good idea of your beneficiary, glance around your notes for words that jump out at you and those that just don't feel right. Your subconscious is watching all this and will give you a sense of what's right, even if it's something you want to consciously dismiss.

You will absolutely know when you're getting close because you'll feel it. Don't worry about how you'll feel; just know it will be obvious. You'll feel an overwhelming sense of relief. Some people offer resistance at this point because they think it's too obvious, but it wasn't obvious before.

You will edit and alter this first draft of your Purpose Statement many times over the coming days. It may take hours or even weeks before it comes together. At first, you may think, "It can't be this; it's too simple; it's too obvious." Disregard that thought. When it does come, it will be obvious and simple. Most great thoughts and ideas are obvious and simple. Every word must fit. If even one word feels wrong, take your statement apart and come at it again until you get it.

Discover Your Passion Project

Here's a self-test to help you discover your own passion project:

- What do you love doing in your free time? Think about the activities that you look forward to and that make you feel energized and fulfilled.
- What are some topics or causes that you care deeply about? This could be anything from environmentalism to social justice to animal welfare.
- What skills do you have that you enjoy using? Consider your strengths and abilities, whether they're technical skills like coding or creative skills like writing or art.
- What are some problems in your community or in the world that you would like to solve? Think about issues that you feel passionate about and would like to contribute to solving.
- What is something that you've always wanted to learn more about or try but haven't had the chance to yet? This could be anything from a new hobby to a

skill you've always been curious about.

After you've answered these questions, look for patterns and connections between your answers. Are there any activities or topics that come up repeatedly? Are there any skills or interests that you could use to contribute to a cause you care about? Use these insights to identify potential passion projects that align with your interests, values, and abilities.

NICHOLAS BOOTHMAN

Acknowledgements

This book owes its existence to the invaluable support and contributions of numerous remarkable individuals who, like unexpected gifts, spontaneously entered my life, ignited paths I never could have foreseen, and then, with some exceptions, faded away again.

Among these amazing individuals are Tim Motion, Jane Somerville, José Prazeres, Andrew Leigh, Dick Martin, Rui Gonçalves, Dorothea Helms, Kerri King, Tim Whyte, Margaret Zwart, Sandra Topper, Ross Harvey, Lynda Hill, and Bernard Scrivener.

Thanks to Alexandra Leggat, my editor, for turning a complex manuscript into an entertaining book.

Additionally, I am thankful to those who supported me with their steadfast patience and unwavering radiance, including Mike Freedman, Dr. Claire Murphy, Arline Smith, Sheldon Rudner, John and Lizzie Blackburn, Roderick Stewart, Jason King, Joanna, Kate, and Pippa Boothman, and Thomas and Sandy Pinto Basto.

And Wendy, of course, who always lights the way.

About the Author

Nicholas Boothman spent more than 35 years studying the ways different people connect and communicate. Today, he is called "one of the leading experts in face-to-face communication in the world" by The New York Times.

He has taught his revolutionary techniques of "Spontaneous Success" to thousands of corporations and colleges and universities around the world including the Harvard and London Business schools. His first two books, How to Make People Like You in 90 Seconds or Less and Convince Them in 90 Seconds or Less have been translated into more than 30 languages.

A former fashion and advertising photographer who dealt with hundreds of new faces a week for clients like AT&T, Revlon and Coca-Cola, he is now recognized as a world-renowned expert in turning chance encounters and unexpected challenges into positive chain reactions.

The New York Times calls him "the new Dale Carnegie," The Economist Magazine calls him "truly inspirational," and Good Morning America says, "His book is my bible!"

www.ingramcontent.com/pod-product-compliance
Lightning Source LLC
Chambersburg PA
CBHW070423010526
44118CB00014B/1875